"This book will make a grea ... repetitive behavior (BFRB) community. Its clear explanation of the comprehensive model for behavioral treatment (ComB) and step-by-step procedural instructions make it a user-friendly guide to reducing hair pulling or skin picking. The principles and methods are brought to life throughout via relatable case descriptions."

> —**David A. F. Haaga, PhD**, professor in the department of psychology at American University, and member of the Scientific Advisory Board of The TLC Foundation for Body-Focused Repetitive Behaviors

"This comprehensive and practical guide to self-care is a godsend for people with BFRBs. The information and treatment techniques offered reflect well the extraordinary wisdom, skill, and down-to-earth styles of the authors, who know as much or more about this topic as anyone in the world. The treatment presented (ComB) is a well-studied, person-centered approach that allows readers to understand their own patterns of behavior and choose from a range of techniques that best match their experiences. Clinical vignettes and plenty of practical material bring this treatment alive for people suffering with BFRBs."

> —**Melinda A. Stanley, PhD**, distinguished emeritus professor in the department of psychiatry and behavioral Sciences at Baylor College of Medicine

"*Overcoming Body-Focused Repetitive Behaviors* is an easy-to-read, step-by-step, self-directed treatment guide. Based on research-supported cognitive behavioral principles, this excellent, practical handbook provides readers with the essentials to understanding their BFRBs, and leads them to discover strategies for implementing effective action plans. Easy-to-use worksheets and intervention strategy lists provide valuable tools for increasing awareness, monitoring experiences, and developing targeted, individualized interventions. A compassionate and empowering writing style and relatable examples offer hope and much-needed support. Readers will undoubtedly benefit from this fundamental, comprehensive self-help guide—a 'must-have' for those struggling with hair pulling, skin picking, nail biting, or other BFRBs."

> —**Marla W. Deibler, PsyD**, founder and executive director at The Center for Emotional Health of Greater Philadelphia, and executive board member and faculty member of the Professional Training Institute (PTI) at The TLC Foundation for Body-Focused Repetitive Behaviors

"An excellent, practical self-help program that brings dignity to those who suffer from BFRBs. It is filled with clinical pearls that come from the authors' years of experience on the forefront of working with and understanding real people with BFRBs. Their commitment to helping sufferers shines through in this tailored approach to each person's unique blend of triggers, and the focus on reaching beyond the condition to the whole person. As a professional, I have relied on their ComB approach for many years, and highly recommend it!"

> —**Aureen Pinto Wagner, PhD**, director of The Anxiety Wellness Center in Cary, NC; and author of *Up and Down the Worry Hill*, *Worried No More*, and *What to Do When Your Child has Obsessive-Compulsive Disorder*

"This is the definitive guide for those who pick or pull. Within these pages, you will first learn the specific challenges that face everyone in your situation. Then you will be guided through concrete steps—the same ones that thousands of people have taken—to win control over your urges, including a 'take-action' attitude that will support you during those tempting times. If you feel overwhelmed by the prospect of taking on your problem—even if you don't feel ready to take action—start by reading this inspiring book."

—**Reid Wilson, PhD**, author of *Stopping the Noise in Your Head*

"A long-awaited gift that did not disappoint. Written in a conversational and compassionate style, the authors share practical information that can help the reader create a customized and comprehensive behavioral plan to best manage their BFRB symptoms. Many helpful ideas and self-awareness tools are shared to offer structure and guidance during this healing journey."

—**Renae Reinardy, PsyD**, director of Lakeside Center for Behavioral Change; project developer for www.couragecritters.com, and board member of The TLC Foundation for Body-Focused Repetitive Behaviors

"This is a much-needed book, written at long last by acknowledged experts with extensive experience. It represents the next wave in BFRB treatment. While comprehensive treatment has been transformative and has been utilized and taught for years, it was not widely accessible to sufferers or clinicians. This book will finally change all that. Countless sufferers will surely benefit from the availability of the know-how this book contains. I will recommend it to everyone, and I give it my highest endorsement."

—**Fred Penzel, PhD**, licensed psychologist with
thirty-eight years' experience in treating BFRBs;
author of *The Hair Pulling Problem*; executive director
of Western Suffolk Psychological Services in
Huntington, NY; and founding member of the
Science Advisory Board of The TLC Foundation for
Body-Focused Repetitive Behaviors

"This is a much-needed, wonderfully written book for anyone who suffers with a BFRB. Written by three experts in the field who are pioneers in the conceptualization and treatment of these often-misunderstood behaviors, it is a clinical triumph! Drawing from decades of experience, the authors provide an easy-to-use, step-by-step guide to help sufferers develop a cutting-edge plan for overcoming their hair pulling or skin picking behavior. The approach is comprehensive, compassionate, and informed by years of clinical wisdom. *Overcoming Body-Focused Repetitive Behaviors* will impact the lives of everyone who reads it."

—**Suzanne Mouton-Odum, PhD**, clinical assistant
professor at Baylor College of Medicine;
director of Psychology Houston, PC; and coauthor
of *A Parent Guide to Hair Pulling Disorder* and
Out of the Rabbit Hole

"Finally! A self-help workbook for BFRBs, authored by three of the professionals most qualified to write it! Stripped of their titles and degrees, Charley, Sherrie, and Ruth introduce themselves with the kind of personal warmth and empathy so prevalent at the TLC retreats. *Overcoming Body-Focused Repetitive Behaviors* is not only a great introduction and review of the ComB model for treating these disorders, but through case examples, homework illustrations, and motivation building, the authors guide the reader through the transformation of this model into a self-tailored treatment program. I highly recommend this book for those who struggle with, live with, or work with BFRBs!"

> —**Allen H. Weg, EdD**, founder and director of Stress and
> Anxiety Services of New Jersey; faculty member of
> The TLC Foundation for Body-Focused Repetitive
> Behaviors' Professional Training Institute (PTI);
> and president of OCD New Jersey, an affiliate of the
> International OCD Foundation

"An incredibly helpful and must-have self-help resource for anyone seeking relief from problematic hair pulling or skin picking. Written by expert clinicians, this highly readable book presents a comprehensive behavioral treatment program (ComB) that addresses the sensory, cognitive, emotional, physical, and environmental aspects of pulling and picking. Accompanying forms and worksheets guide readers through clearly described treatment steps, which are also illustrated by a series of informative case examples. Additional chapters provide valuable information about increasing treatment motivation, maintaining treatment gains, and managing hair, skin, and nail health."

> —**John Piacentini, PhD, ABPP**, professor of psychiatry at
> the UCLA Semel Institute for Neuroscience and Human
> Behavior, and director of the Semel Institute's Child OCD,
> Anxiety, and Tic Disorders Program Clinic

"This book is an incredible contribution to the field. Every therapist, physician's office, dermatologist, cosmetologist, and psychiatrist should run out and buy this invaluable resource. These world-class specialist authors have taken their decades of experience and put it into a detailed how-to manual for people suffering from a BFRB. Those who are struggling with pulling their hair or picking their skin, and want to know what to do, will find a wealth of information, practical steps, science, and strategies they can use. This book helps people understand their own very individual patterns of behavior so that they can create a personalized plan that will work for them. They will also find compassion, warmth, and a deep understanding of what it is like to live with a BFRB. It is destigmatizing, and will reduce the shame and loneliness that so many people experience. I love this book."

—**Shaw Welch, PhD**, cofounder of Evidence Based Treatment Centers of Seattle, director of the Child Anxiety Center of Seattle, and affiliate assistant professor in the department of psychology at the University of Washington

Overcoming Body-Focused Repetitive Behaviors

A COMPREHENSIVE BEHAVIORAL TREATMENT *for* HAIR PULLING *and* SKIN PICKING

CHARLES S. MANSUETO, PhD

SHERRIE MANSFIELD VAVRICHEK, LCSW-C

RUTH GOLDFINGER GOLOMB, LCPC

New Harbinger Publications, Inc.

Publisher's Note

NEW HARBINGER PUBLICATIONS is a registered trademark of New Harbinger Publications, Inc.

Distributed in Canada by Raincoast Books

Copyright © 2019 by Charles S. Mansueto, Sherrie Mansfield Vavrichek, and Ruth Golomb
New Harbinger Publications, Inc.
5674 Shattuck Avenue
Oakland, CA 94609
www.newharbinger.com

Cover design by Amy Daniel

Acquired by Wendy Millstine

Edited by Ken Knabb

All Rights Reserved

FSC
www.fsc.org
MIX
Paper from responsible sources
FSC® C011935

Library of Congress Cataloging-in-Publication Data on file

Printed in the United States of America

23   22   21

10   9   8   7   6   5   4

This book is dedicated to all individuals with BFRBs, and especially the thousands who have trusted us with their personal stories. You have been and remain a source of inspiration to us every single day.

Contents

Foreword

Let's be clear, the authors of this book are rock stars. And not just because they'll give their all to a night of karaoke (which they absolutely will). Charley, Ruth, and Sherrie are beloved by their peers and patients alike because their unsurpassed clinical expertise is matched by their devotion to our community. When you talk with each of them, you feel understood as a full-blown *human*, not a disorder. For a person with a body-focused repetitive behavior (BFRB) like you and me, that understanding is a rare gift. I believe that is the feeling you will have as you read this book.

It is also the key to the effectiveness of the Comprehensive Behavioral (ComB) treatment of BFRBs addressed in these pages. ComB is founded on the need to understand you, and your unique experience of a BFRB, first, and to tailor treatment interventions to your specific combination of feelings, thoughts, environment, sensations, and patterns.

The void into which the authors stepped as they began to develop the ComB approach can't be overstated. We now know that at least one in fifty people lives with a BFRB. Thirty years ago, hair pulling or skin picking were little-known problems, and shame led the people suffering with them to do everything they could to be invisible.

I began pulling out my eyelashes as a child in the early 1980s. My eyelids were often bare, and my eyebrows scraggly. I was blessed to have gentle, loving parents who did everything they could to be my allies in my efforts to stop pulling. But even with that support, I couldn't help but feel hopeless, ugly, and ashamed of my "gross" urge to pull, and of my repeated failure to stop. I made resolution after resolution. I wore oven mitts to block my hands. Smeared petroleum jelly all over my eyebrows. Tied my hands to my waist. Cut the calluses off my fingers so that it would hurt to pull. You've probably tried some of these failed "self-help" approaches, and more. Yet looking back, I feel lucky that no one knew enough to diagnose me as having trichotillomania at that time, because any treatment prescribed in that era would have been ineffective or worse.

I became involved with the TLC Foundation for Body-Focused Repetitive Behaviors nearly twenty-five years ago, and met Charley, Ruth, Sherrie, and a small band of dedicated clinicians and researchers. What I witnessed in those early days was a unique collaboration between clinicians and those of us affected by BFRBs. *We learned from each other.* Christina Pearson, who founded TLC, deliberately created an environment at her rustic retreats that leveled the playing field between expert and lay person. Doctors and patients alike, we were all out of our comfort zone in the woods. We shared our stories around the campfire. We shed our shame and took off our wigs and makeup. And, yes, we sang karaoke.

It takes a special therapist to be not just willing, but eager, to participate in that kind of nonhierarchical environment. Through these interactions, and by listening to the thousands of patients they have helped at the Behavior Therapy Center of Greater Washington, the authors became intimately familiar with how we experience hair pulling and skin picking, and the many other types of body-focused repetitive behaviors, from nose picking to nail biting.

It is an immense relief to meet other people who share your problem, whatever it is. This is particularly true of body-focused repetitive behaviors. Many of us have suffered for decades, thinking we are the only ones who do this strange behavior. I remember how life-changing it felt to first read an essay by another hair-puller and realize that we shared the same ritual of feeling for a coarse hair, plucking it, and pressing it against our lips.

But by listening to thousands of people talk about hair pulling and skin picking, you come to understand that though we share many traits, we have just as many differences. We pull or pick from different places. We are driven by varying emotions. We bite the roots or don't. We pick wide awake in front of a mirror, or in the dark when we are falling asleep. It feels good. It hurts. Or both. We are each unique. Charley, Ruth, and Sherrie recognized early on that these differences were important. They realized that the details of how we pull and pick are vital to good treatment. They built a treatment model that personalizes therapy.

Thank goodness they have now translated ComB to a self-help format! Despite enormous progress in recent years, these disorders are far from household terms and there are far too few therapists specializing in this field. Charley, Ruth, and Sherrie have made a tremendous contribution by training many young therapists in the ComB model, both at their successful clinic and by developing and serving as faculty for the Professional Training Institutes run by TLC. Yet lack of access to appropriate therapy is a critical problem for most of us living with BFRBs. I expect this book to be a key new tool in our arsenal.

Since I first joined TLC and met the authors of this book, I have had decades of recovery from my hair pulling. I can't say the impulse to pull and pick has totally disappeared, but I have the concepts that help me understand my urges, and tools that enable me to keep them in check.

My eleven-year-old daughter is now struggling with her own BFRB. Charley, Ruth, and Sherrie have done as much as anyone to create a better world for her. We don't have all the answers yet. But thanks in large part to their work, we do have helpful treatment, and an understanding that BFRBs don't have to be shameful—we're all human and we are in it together.

—Jennifer Raikes
Executive Director
TLC Foundation for Body-Focused
Repetitive Behaviors

Introduction

If you are reading this book, it is likely that your life has been affected by a *body-focused repetitive behavior* (BFRB). Most people don't even know what that is, but *you* know. If you have experienced it in isolation, you may have lived for years thinking that you were alone, but now you know that you are not.

Just like every other human being, you have your problems, many of which result in pain and suffering. But as someone who has a picking or pulling disorder, you have the double whammy of not only suffering from the disorder, but of being held responsible for bringing it on yourself. That judgmental perspective is not unique to BFRBs—think of how people feel about addictions, for example—but it is an aspect of the BFRB experience that can contribute to the disruption of relationships, career aspirations, and self-esteem, and that ultimately can cause the hope for a high quality of life to slip further and further away. Secrecy and deceit can replace openness and connectedness as ways of life. And there is the ever-present companion—shame—tearing away at efforts to repair the physical and emotional damage and to restore self-pride.

A case can be made for coming to terms with and perhaps accepting a life with a BFRB as a constant companion. After all, no one is perfect, and isn't it true that we all have strengths and weaknesses, advantages and disadvantages, and qualities both admirable and disconcerting? Aren't we all living a life in which we are striving to minimize our liabilities and capitalize on our strengths? So why not simply accept the fact that you have a BFRB and stop worrying about it?

We will not oppose that argument. After all, we know that you are a unique person who is so much more than your problems. We know that you are three-dimensional, a person with qualities, capabilities, and talents, who happens to also have a BFRB, and we hope that you know it, too. However, because you are reading this book, we believe that some significant part of you still hopes for a life free from your BFRB. Even without that problem, there will of course be challenges to face—life can be very difficult, even for people who seem to have many obvious advantages. But if the energies that are drained by living with hair pulling and skin picking can be released for other purposes, perhaps a proportion of suffering can be transformed into energy directed toward living well.

The authors of this book collectively have devoted more than seventy-five years to professional involvement with BFRB sufferers, families, therapists, and researchers. This book enables us to share with you the fruits of our experiences in the hope that they will serve you well. In it, we have distilled what we have learned during this time into a self-help program that we believe will offer you the power to fight back and win the battle with BFRBs.

THE BEGINNINGS

Our involvement with trichotillomania (TTM) and the creation of the Comprehensive Behavioral (ComB) approach has been a remarkable journey for us, and we want to share a bit of our history, because it has closely coincided with the history of modern efforts to find solutions for these very human problems.

The years seem to have flown by. It was almost thirty years ago, 1990 to be exact, when the three of us were on a plane bound for San Francisco, on our way to present what we were to learn later was the first national symposium on TTM, a disorder that was little known at the time and thought to be quite rare and rather exotic. Our connection with TTM began with Charley's involvement with the researchers at the National Institute of Mental Health (NIMH) on projects to detect brain changes and improvements in symptoms in subjects treated for obsessive compulsive disorder (OCD).

Some of the subjects who volunteered were people who struggled with irresistible and recurring patterns of pulling out their own hair. Thinking that those people were possibly a subtype of OCD, the researchers invited them to participate in a smaller study designed to test the effectiveness of a promising OCD medication on this specific condition. Unfortunately, results showed that the medication was nowhere near as effective for helping with TTM as it was for OCD. Among those who had not received relief were around forty disappointed people who wanted more help. So the researchers referred those people to Charley. The researchers were aware that he was the director of the Behavior Therapy Center of Greater Washington, and they knew of the Center's success in treating OCD with cognitive behavior therapy (CBT). They wondered if CBT, a learning-based approach, might help those with hair pulling as well.

Charley enlisted the aid of his colleagues in the practice, Ruth and Sherrie, to see if CBT would work for this population. The trouble was that, like virtually all researchers and clinicians at the time, we were largely in the dark about this mostly ignored problem. The large number of persons who pulled out their hair and who responded to NIMH's search for research subjects was an early clue that this problem was not as rare as had been thought. In fact, later studies showed that as many as one in fifty people have experienced this disorder at some point in their lives—that's over six and a half million people in the United States alone.

Having forty individuals with TTM was a golden opportunity to learn more about the problem and to explore possible ways to help those people. The first treatment we tried was a therapy technique that had been around since the early 1970s called Habit Reversal Training (HRT). This had been reported to be a successful treatment for a broad range of "nervous habits," including TTM, in a few early studies. Essentially, it taught people with problem behavior patterns to practice actions that were incompatible with movements that were used in performance of their nervous habit. For hair pulling this might mean squeezing the hands into a fist while holding them away from hairs that might otherwise be pulled out. We applied HRT with due diligence, but many of our hair pullers were unhappy with this treatment. Some had tried it before with minimal success, and some said it seemed to them to be a "white knuckle" approach that pitted willpower against impossibly strong urges. The general feeling was that it offered too simplistic a solution for such a deeply ingrained behavior. While our patients gave it their best effort, it became clear to us that HRT as described in the literature was not adequate for the job.

We realized we had to do more, and that began the search for a better understanding of TTM and the quest for a new and effective treatment for that problem. The information gathered from this remarkable group of patients provided a new and compelling picture of the disorder. So much valuable information was forthcoming that it required organization into a broadened perspective on the many factors that caused TTM to enmesh itself so deeply in each sufferer's experience. The ComB model of TTM was created to serve this purpose. More importantly, this opened the door to development of ComB treatment for TTM and the related problems that are now called BFRBs. As we gained confidence in the usefulness of ComB, it made sense to share it with the professional community, and this is what led us to our symposium in San Francisco.

So, what *was* the information presented at the San Francisco symposium and how did it come to mark the beginning of dramatic breakthroughs in the understanding and treatment of TTM and similar problems? Charley's presentation offered a sharply focused description of what actually happened in the process of hair pulling, including many details that had never before been described in professional accounts: the physical aspects of hair pulling as well as the internal experiences—thoughts, emotions, beliefs, and sensations—of the individual. In addition, he introduced the new ComB treatment approach that took into account and addressed hair pulling's newfound complexity, and the unique ways this was expressed in each individual. Ruth described how the treatment derived from this approach was used in both individual and group formats. Results from our early research efforts demonstrated that the ComB approach held much promise as an effective treatment for this tenacious problem in our clinical setting. Finally, Sherrie reported on the results of the above-mentioned NIMH study, which showed that the experimental drug, while it did help some hair pulling individuals to some extent, was by no means a magic bullet and was not a reliable solution. As the search for effective medical treatment for BFRBs has continued, ComB treatment has proven to be a viable alternative.

BUT WAIT, THERE'S MORE

In a nutshell, those were some of the findings presented at our symposium, but something else happened in that room on that day that is perhaps the most amazing part of the story. Attendees included the usual array of therapists and researchers—though the group was larger than we had expected and we were pleased to see that there were many notable researchers and clinicians in attendance. Also present in the audience was Christina Pearson, the founder and head of a newly formed grassroots organization called the Trichotillomania Learning Center (now called TLC: The Foundation for Body-Focused Repetitive Behaviors). Christina's organization, we would learn, was devoted to serving the needs of hair pullers and skin pickers worldwide. A decades-long sufferer of TTM and skin picking disorder, she would become the true, life force behind the modern efforts to reach out to sufferers of these disorders and to inspire professional efforts to understand and treat them effectively.

Christina lived not far from San Francisco, in Santa Cruz, California, and it was there that she and a few other women who had joined her in the cause learned of our upcoming symposium in San Francisco and decided to attend. She frequently has shared her experience of being shocked and deeply moved to find that there were therapists and researchers who were actually interested in solving the problems she had experienced firsthand. What she had heard at that symposium made sense to her.

After the presentations ended and the discussions died down, Christina rose from her seat, identified herself, described her organization, and challenged the therapists and researchers in the room to join her in her efforts. A number did step up—including all three of us—and the professional wing of TLC was born. At that meeting, in that room, the events of the day were to mark the end of the "Dark Ages" and the dawn of the "Age of Enlightenment" for hair pulling, skin picking, and a cluster of related problems experts now referred to as "body-focused repetitive behaviors," or BFRBs.

The decades that followed the symposium have been remarkable ones for the world of BFRBs. From that point to the present there have been ever-increasing scientific efforts to understand these disorders, to treat the sufferers, to prevent the problems from occurring whenever possible, and to get the word out so that no one ever need suffer secretly, in shamed silence, thinking that they are the only one so afflicted.

Over the past thirty years we have been active in the field and have watched it blossom, as research efforts and clinical interest in BFRBs have grown by leaps and bounds. During this time, the American Psychiatric Association has appropriately improved the criteria for TTM and approved an alternative name—Hair Pulling Disorder. And Skin Picking (Excoriation) Disorder is now included as a legitimate diagnosis in the new diagnostic category of "Obsessive-Compulsive and Related Disorders," along with HPD. To the greatest degree these are direct results of the efforts of TLC—Christina, the TLC staff and volunteers, the involved professionals, and the sufferers and their loved ones who have joined the cause.

The ComB approach has played a major role in the exciting developments over the last three decades, and ComB treatment has been recognized by TLC and its Scientific Advisory Board as a gold standard for TTM and other BFRBs. As such, it is the model used by TLC's Professional Training Institute to train BFRB therapists, and it has been widely used in TLC's efforts to educate the public as well as professionals about the nature and treatment of BFRBs. In addition, ComB has been described in numerous professional publications and has been taught at hundreds of TLC-sponsored retreats, conferences, and programs.

Although it has been tweaked and expanded over the years, the approach we use and teach today is substantially the same approach that we first unveiled almost thirty years ago. During this time we have received numerous requests to write a detailed, step-by-step book so that anyone, anywhere, can use it as a guide to their recovery from skin picking or hair pulling problems. This book is our response to those requests. So now, for the first time, we offer you, dear reader, ComB in a self-help form. This method has helped many others to manage and overcome their BFRB problems. We sincerely hope it will enable you to do the same.

—Charles Mansueto, Sherrie Vavrichek, Ruth Golomb

PART 1

Getting Started

CHAPTER 1

Hair Pulling and Skin Picking Disorders: The Basics

It is probably safe to say that as long as people have had skin, they've picked at it, and as long as they've had hair, they've pulled at it. If you engage excessively in one or both of these activities, you might have only recently found out that your condition has a name. Although the terms "trichotillomania" and "excoriation disorder" are still used, the more straightforward terms "hair pulling disorder" and "skin picking disorder" are now widely accepted as alternative psychiatric terminology, and the term "body-focused repetitive behaviors" (BFRBs) is often used when referring to these and similar behaviors. For the remainder of this book we will use the abbreviations HPD and SPD to refer to the two specific disorders, and BFRBs to refer to such behaviors in general. In this chapter we will cover some basic information about HPD and SPD and provide a brief overview of the state of knowledge about these conditions.

WHAT IS HAIR PULLING DISORDER (HPD)?

If you have HPD it means that you repetitively engage in hair pulling that produces damage and hair loss to your scalp or to other areas of your body. It also causes you to experience significant distress and may interfere with aspects of your day-to-day life. Perhaps you pull hair from your scalp, since that is most common, but you may also pull from your eyebrows, eyelashes, pubic hair, or any other body hair. Maybe you use your fingers to pull, but you may use implements such as tweezers, pins, or other devices. Your pulling episodes may be sporadic or almost constant and may occupy just seconds or up to hours of the day. Perhaps, like most other sufferers, you feel that your hair pulling is out of control, and you are distressed by the cosmetic damage it produces. HPD may also have a negative impact on your personal sense of well-being, productivity, and relationships with others. The personal toll it takes on you in terms of social and emotional consequences may range from mild to severe, and it may be disproportionate to the extent of your actual cosmetic damage.

Perhaps your life has been terribly altered by your BFRB, resulting in shame, embarrassment, low self-esteem, anxiety, depression, isolation, or feelings of unattractiveness. And your efforts to conceal the physical damage may have led to a life of secrecy and concealment—using makeup, hairstyles, clothing, wigs, and other devices designed to camouflage the physical results of your pulling. Like many others, you might also avoid ordinary, everyday activities and simple pleasures such as swimming, sexual intimacy, bright lights, windy conditions, and even routine visits to hairdressers, optometrists, or physicians, out of fear that your damaging activities will be discovered. Even your ability to function efficiently in school or in the workplace may be jeopardized. Perhaps, on the other hand, your HPD has less severe personal consequences for you, but you just want to stop and haven't been able to do so.

While it was once thought to be very rare, current estimates suggest that HPD occurs in 3% to 6% of the general population, with women outnumbering men by about nine to one. Most commonly, problem hair pulling begins around the time of puberty, but smaller numbers of individuals begin pulling in infancy, childhood, or sometimes into adulthood. Your disorder most likely has been a chronic condition that has waxed and waned in severity over the years.

WHAT IS SKIN PICKING DISORDER (SPD)?

Similarly, SPD refers to recurrent picking or squeezing of the skin that causes significant damage to skin tissue. Like others, you may pick or squeeze at the site of blemishes or other irregularities such as scabs, insect bites, pimples, and rough, dry, or loose patches of skin. Your recurrent picking may cause you significant distress or interference with important daily activities. Any area of the body—face, torso, arms and hands, legs and feet, or combinations of these—may be targeted for picking, usually with fingers and fingernails, but sometimes with implements such as pins or tweezers being employed. Skin picking has much in common with hair pulling. You may spend hours each day picking your skin in a manner that feels compulsive and irresistible. In some cases, the cosmetic damage is extreme, even requiring plastic surgery. In other cases the damage may be almost imperceptible to others. However severe your problem is, we know that it can bring with it the same variety of personal and social tolls that is seen among hair pullers. Just how common SPD is in the general population is not clear, but estimates ranging from 1% to 6% have been reported by researchers. SPD, like HPD, is considered to be a chronic condition that fluctuates in severity over time. It, too, is seen more commonly in women than in men. If your skin picking began when you were a teen, you are among the majority of people with SPD. For some individuals, however, skin picking can begin in childhood or in adulthood.

WHY DO PEOPLE DEVELOP HAIR PULLING AND SKIN PICKING DISORDERS?

You may have asked yourself this simple question: Why on earth do I do these things to myself? It's a reasonable question and it deserves an answer. Unfortunately, everyone, professionals and sufferers alike, must accept the fact that at this time we simply don't have a satisfying answer to that important and fundamental question. What we do have is a number of informed guesses, some more promising than others, that attempt to provide the answer or at least part of the answer to that question. It should be acknowledged that hair pulling or skin picking is not the exclusive domain of people with disorders. While most of us like to present a respectable façade to our fellow human beings, in many of our private moments we reveal ourselves as the pickers, scratchers, nibblers, pullers, and biters that we are. So why is it that some people cross the line and get into real problems with such common practices while most don't? For our purposes we will group the possible answers under two general headings: *Biological Theories* and *Learning Theories*, while recognizing that we are grouping quite different approaches under each general heading. As we shall see, the various theories are not necessarily mutually exclusive. It may be that a combination of ingredients among those identified in the various theories may actually operate to fuel these self-damaging practices.

Biological Theories

Scientists interested in possible biological contributions to these disorders have approached them from a variety of perspectives. Some have pursued the idea that certain people inherited a kind of inborn genetic plan, like a computer program, that makes them vulnerable to these sorts of problems. It is true that hair pulling and skin picking problems do seem to occur within families more than chance alone would allow. So far, however, no particular gene or sets of genes have been discovered that carry the plans for hair pulling or skin picking into the next generation.

Some scientists have explored the idea that these types of disorders are related to grooming patterns that are seen throughout many members of the animal kingdom. In this view, hair pulling and skin picking can be considered healthy grooming behaviors that have gotten out of control. Interestingly, there are examples of animal behavior that seem to involve unhealthy and self-damaging grooming patterns. Some dogs, cats, rodents, and other animals damage their skin and hair through excessive grooming and some birds have been known to pull out their own feathers and damage their skin. It is possible that researchers studying such behaviors in animals may find clues to the biological origins of these disorders, possibly leading to better treatment or preventive approaches.

Other biology-minded scientists are looking into activities within the brain and nervous system to discover what might underlie HPD and SPD at the brain and nervous system level. These scientists are investigating the possibility that there are malfunctions in the chemistry, structure, or functioning of circuits within the nervous system that may be responsible for repetitive, self-damaging behavior patterns. Recent technological breakthroughs, such as brain imaging, have enabled scientists to study these physical structures as well as the functioning of the living human brain with clarity and precision that was impossible to achieve even a short time ago. These researchers search for abnormalities in the physical makeup of the brain, or in the way that different systems or circuits of the brain communicate in controlling complex human functioning. This work, however, is in its relative infancy and has yet to offer any definitive clues as to the origins of BFRBs.

On another front, many scientists have focused on chemicals found throughout the brain and nervous system called neurotransmitters, which are necessary for the transmission of signals throughout the body and are essential for life. The possibility that certain of these chemicals may not be regulated properly, and thus may be involved in human disorders involving unwanted repetitive behaviors, has spurred a great deal of attention. If chemical malfunctions could be identified for skin picking and hair pulling, medications designed to adjust and regulate the identified neurotransmitters might bring an end to the suffering caused by these disorders. Perhaps you have sought help for your condition, hoping for a medication that will cure you. Unfortunately, as of yet no chemical malfunctions have been found to be associated with BFRBs, and no medications designed to regulate specific neurotransmitters have been found effective for treating any BFRB. However, the search goes on, and the use of medications in BFRB treatment will be addressed later.

Learning Theories

Theoretical models emphasizing learning take a wide variety of forms. While earlier theories viewed hair-pulling and skin-picking problems as symptoms of deep disturbance within the individual, learning models regard these repetitive behavior patterns as *the problem* rather than as a symptom of some hidden disruption. In general, these approaches emphasize processes of learning and repeated practice as essential for understanding and treating these disorders. When the focus is broadened to include distorted thinking and thoughts that facilitate the destructive behavior patterns found in BFRBs, these models are termed "cognitive behavioral" models. Generally, cognitive behavior therapy (CBT) emphasizes the interaction between feelings, thoughts, and behaviors that are involved in psychological problems, including BFRBs. There are three influential approaches to understanding BFRBs from a behavioral or cognitive behavioral prospective that have led to the development of promising treatments.

Azrin's Behavioral Model: An early and very influential effort to explain a cluster of problems from a behavioral perspective was reported by Nathan Azrin and Gregory Nunn (1973). In their view, certain disorders involving repetitive behaviors, such as tics, nail biting, and hair pulling, were considered "nervous habits" that are performed in response to tension and stress. They suggested that movements associated with these problems become connected to, and triggered by, many situations that the person encounters, as well as by feelings and sensations, especially anxiety, occurring within that person. Because of these connections, and through extensive repetition, the individual becomes largely unaware that the behaviors are actually being performed, and thus, through practice, they become almost entirely automatic and beyond the individual's conscious control. This view led Azrin and his colleagues to develop a treatment approach called Habit Reversal Therapy (HRT), designed to be applied to problems within the identified cluster of "nervous habits," including HPD.

Because hair pulling was considered to be a learned, well-practiced, automatic set of movements linked with large numbers of external situations and internal cues, HRT employed two key treatment components: "awareness training" (designed to bring the problem into conscious awareness) and "competing response training." This latter is the hallmark component of HRT, in which behaviors incompatible with the problem behaviors are practiced that interfere with the problem behaviors and thus weaken them over time. This is accomplished by a technique designed to strengthen motor habits (well-practiced movements) that are incompatible with the problem behaviors, such as clenching your fists whenever you feel the urge to pull your hair.

In various later publications, Azrin and his colleagues added a number of other treatment components to HRT, including relaxation training, imaginal rehearsal, and social support. Early reports examining the effectiveness of HRT were very encouraging; however, later ones were less so with regard to the effectiveness and durability of HRT. Nonetheless, it should be noted that, to date, HRT-based therapy has received more support from clinical research studies than any other single form of treatment.

"HRT Plus" Models: Recognizing the likelihood that Azrin's behavioral model oversimplified the nature of the BFRBs by failing to identify critical elements that instigate and maintain these problematic patterns of behavior, some other researchers have proposed a number of additional factors that they believed might be important for understanding and effectively treating these problems. If you have recently been in HRT-based therapy, your therapist might have felt that you should consider additional factors contributing to your problem, such as environmental cues or unhelpful thoughts that trigger your BFRBs. Or your therapist may have focused on the possibility that hair pulling and skin picking represent misguided mechanisms to reduce and control a variety of unwanted emotions and other uncomfortable internal experiences. New theories have influenced clinical practice, and efforts to enhance HRT treatment for

BFRBs now typically involve adding new elements to various combinations of HRT components. Recent HRT-based treatments for BFRBs reported in the literature thus often consist of HRT *plus* stimulus-control techniques, HRT *plus* cognitive therapy, or HRT *plus* any one of several emotional self-regulation strategies. Research reports tend to show that these types of treatments derived from cognitive behavioral models benefit many people for whom they are employed, at least to some degree.

The Comprehensive Behavioral Model (ComB): This conceptual model, published in 1997 by Charles Mansueto, Amanda Thomas, Ruth Stemberger, and Ruth Golomb, was the first to address the full complexity of BFRBs and to suggest a variety of avenues for the development of more effective treatments. That article provided a detailed description of the many ways that various behavioral, cognitive, and affective (emotional) variables can be linked interactively to foster and maintain hair pulling or skin picking. This approach highlights a wide variety of internal and external triggers that serve to jumpstart picking or pulling, and it also identifies specific learning mechanisms by which the outcome of those behaviors reinforces and thereby strengthens and perpetuates the problems. While the details of the ComB theoretical model are not essential for our purposes here, they have been clearly laid out in a variety of scientific publications for over two decades. What is important for you to know is that the ComB treatment approach can give you, as it has already done for many others, the tools to change entrenched behavior patterns and to modify the thoughts and feelings that have fueled your hair pulling or skin picking for too long.

COMB TREATMENT

As described in the professional literature, ComB treatment begins by employing a structured, in-depth assessment to identify the unique pattern of sensory (sensations), cognitive (thoughts), affective (feelings), motor (movements), and place (environmental) factors that serve to trigger and maintain BFRB. Then an individualized treatment plan can be developed with the goal of providing self-management techniques matched to individual needs, thus enabling increased control over your problem. The program is designed to interrupt ongoing problem behaviors and to provide nonharmful alternative mechanisms to help address the habits, emotions, and thoughts or beliefs that drive individuals to damage their hair or skin. This is accomplished by meeting each person's unique needs in other, healthier ways.

Research designed to test the overall effectiveness of ComB treatment for BFRBs is currently underway. However, it is worth noting that all of the key elements of ComB treatment are based on theoretically sound, research-supported clinical techniques examined in numerous research studies and used by thousands of cognitive behavior therapists worldwide to treat a broad range of disorders. Decades of experience by scores of expert clinicians utilizing ComB treatment for BFRBs suggests that this approach has many advantages over other existing treatment approaches. Building on this research and experience, ComB can guide the discovery of your BFRB profile and help organize this information into familiar categories of human experience, including the cognitive and sensory modalities that are absent from, or peripheral to, other treatment approaches. Perhaps most importantly, ComB helps generate a broad and almost endless array of possible therapeutic interventions and will allow you to choose among these possibilities to ensure a good fit between your individual preferences and the techniques that you choose to employ in your recovery.

Here, for the first time in written form, the ComB treatment program is offered as a self-help approach for ending the twin scourges of hair pulling and skin picking disorders. In the following chapters you will be guided through the steps as if you had an expert treatment provider by your side. We encourage you to make full use of these techniques, which have provided relief to thousands of BFRB sufferers. We wish you the best on your journey!

CHAPTER 2

Preparing for Change

Are you ready to take on your BFRB? It is such a simple question, but one that is not always easy to answer. While each person's situation is unique, and the answer can be complex, there are telltale signs of readiness. One of the first is an interest in learning more. The fact that you have picked up this book and read it up to this point is a sign of hope—a key ingredient for this or any recovery process.

In this chapter we will ask you to consider your life in a broader perspective before moving on to the design of your personal recovery plan. There is probably never a perfect time to make major life changes, and even with excellent planning, unforeseen circumstances can threaten our best efforts. Because significant efforts for self-improvement are rarely easy, we ask you to first reflect on potential obstacles to success; to identify them so you can clear the way as best you can.

GETTING READY FOR CHANGE

We might all wish that hair-pulling and skin-picking problems would just go away on their own. But the reality is that effort, focus, and perseverance are required. And it is also true that various factors can complicate and undermine the process of recovery, despite the best laid plans. These can include internal obstacles, such as unhelpful emotions and beliefs arising from within ourselves. External obstacles, generated by factors such as work or family obligations, can also undermine our best efforts. This can be especially true for individuals who lead busy, stressful lives and who may question whether or not they have the time or energy to devote to the process of recovery.

So how do you go about making this time the *right* time? How can you minimize the impact of obstacles, whether they are external or internal? What about the obstacles you are unable to address right now? In the rest of this chapter you will find some typical challenges that have the potential to interfere with "getting out of the gate," as well as some recommendations for managing them. Although everyone's situation is unique, try to see whether you can identify any circumstances that are similar to those in your own life, and whether the suggestions offered might help you generate your own tactics for managing your BFRB .

INTERNAL CHALLENGES: COGNITIVE AND EMOTIONAL OBSTACLES

We encourage you to cultivate an attitude of hope and curiosity about the process of recovery. Yet an individual's internal experiences can wreak havoc on plans for change. These kinds of unhelpful internal experiences include thoughts, beliefs, and emotions. Factors such as these can interact in complex ways and do much harm. You have little to lose and much to gain by honestly assessing problematic thoughts, beliefs, and emotions so that you are better prepared to address them as they arise.

Dealing with Secrets and Shame

Perhaps the greatest source of emotional pain for people with BFRBs is shame, and the belief that usually accompanies it—that the problem reflects a weakness of character. Such individuals assume that if others were to become aware of their picking or pulling, they would be rejected or thought of as a "weird," "crazy," or "disgusting," so they live a life of secrecy. But this can make things worse for the secret keepers, adding to their burden and depriving them of a potential support system. Furthermore, the isolation that results can generate and deepen other harmful factors such as anxiety, depression, and poor self-esteem, which in turn can worsen picking or pulling, and thus create a vicious cycle of suffering.

If this problem feels familiar to you, we understand that for many people it takes courage to risk disclosing. But if it seems within your range of possibilities, consider confiding in a trusted family member or friend about your condition. Many of our clients with BFRBs have done so, and the vast majority have been pleasantly surprised to learn that their confidants responded in a caring and supportive way. If you take the chance and put your trust in someone, you may begin to feel the lifting of an emotional load and the freeing up of energy that can then be directed toward useful ends.

The support role played by others will vary according to circumstances and preferences. Be clear in your own mind about what you might need or want from your support network. If you are fortunate enough to have a person who wants to help, communicate your preferences as specifically as possible. Perhaps a daily check-in phone call may help maintain your spirits and motivation. Or maybe you will want them to just "be there" when you need someone to lean on. Your situation may vary from week to week, so request changes along the way if you feel that your needs have changed. And don't forget to express your appreciation and offer to reciprocate should the need arise.

Of course, it is important to be careful when deciding with whom to share this personal information. Once the genie is out of the bottle, you can't put it back in.

If you feel that disclosure of this sort is not appropriate to your circumstances, you may find more anonymous ways to share your personal information with others and gain support in the process— through local support groups. You may already be familiar with groups that help people lose weight, control alcohol consumption, or increase the time they spend exercising. Likewise, connecting with others may be quite helpful in recovering from your skin picking or hair pulling. Like many others, you may find that group support can be especially valuable when your commitment to the change process is flagging. In addition, support groups give people the opportunity to give as well as receive, a process that benefits everyone. TLC: The Foundation for Body-Focused Behavior Disorders, keeps a list of BFRB support groups meeting around the country, as well as providing information about starting your own group.

TLC also provides resources for those who are looking for more anonymous ways to share personal information with others, either in addition to—or instead of—talking with people who are close to them. It can serve as a virtual source of support to you through its website, through informative and inspirational articles in its newsletter, through online webinars, and through in-person events, including an annual conference and one-day workshops around the country. Christina Pearson, founder and former director of TLC, conducts retreats for BFRB sufferers through her Heart and Soul Academy and helps individuals connect with each other and with knowledgeable professionals through her website. Keep these valuable resources in mind as you move through your self-help program, as they are only a few key taps away.

Dealing with Your Own Unhelpful Beliefs

There are two widespread but mistaken beliefs about BFRBs that can interfere with readiness for change. One is that pulling and picking are such mysterious behaviors that they cannot be understood and are beyond control. If you hold this belief, reading this book and following the ComB program should go a long way toward correcting this misconception by demystifying BFRBs. Furthermore, involvement with TLC can provide the kind of accurate information to put this idea to rest for good.

The other belief, quite the opposite of what was just discussed, is that a picking or pulling problem should have a simple and easy solution, and once found, shouldn't require hard work to overcome it. If you have the belief that recovery will be easy once you learn the "secret" to stopping, remember that your BFRB has been a well-practiced routine, most likely for years. Moreover, certain needs are being met by these practices or they would not have continued. Accepting the reality that this is not a simple problem, and that it is unlikely to yield to a simple solution, will allow you to acquire more realistic expectations. These, in turn, will help you to be patient and persistent in your efforts, even when the inevitable setbacks occur. Plan to celebrate small successes and to find ways to acknowledge your progress, reward your efforts, and do whatever you can to bolster your motivation. Keep in mind that longstanding behavior patterns will take time and effort to change, and that in the case of BFRBs, patience, commitment, and flexibility are key ingredients for success.

EXTERNAL CHALLENGES: OBLIGATIONS TO OTHERS

Modern life can be busy, and our obligations have a way of demanding great attention, sometimes at the most inconvenient times. You may think that there is little room in your life for making efforts above and beyond those that are required for family, work, or school. But in fact, as your skin picking or hair pulling decreases, you will actually have more time and emotional energy to manage those obligations. So think of the time and effort you put into your recovery as an investment, one that will increase your level of productive functioning in the world, in addition to improving your health and personal well-being.

Preparing for your recovery will involve assessing your commitments and obligations. If it is possible to do so, you may want to adjust, ratchet back, or let go of some aspects of your responsibilities, especially those that encourage or otherwise drive your picking or pulling. Toughing it out may be desirable at times, and even necessary in some circumstances, but during your recovery period you will need to be careful not to overextend yourself in ways that create more stress than you can handle.

Managing Life Stressors

While some stress is an inevitable part of life, excessive stress can be debilitating, so it is worth incorporating into your life activities that are known to help reduce stress, aid relaxation, and contribute to a positive sense of well-being. Tried and true methods that have stood the test of time include meditation, warm baths, breathing exercises, yoga, and, for some, prayer. Everyday activities that may serve similar purposes include working on crossword puzzles, listening to music, going out with friends, going for walks, or engaging in activities that connect us with nature. Our clients who have chosen to incorporate activities such as these into their schedule on a regular basis have reported surprisingly powerful benefits.

A number of the activities mentioned above include some degree of physical exercise. We all know that exercise—a well-documented method of reducing stress—can feel good and is good for us when done properly. In addition to being a stress-buster, exercise helps our body function at an optimal level, releases chemicals in the brain that contribute to feelings of well-being, and helps us sleep better. If you currently do not engage in physical exercise on a regular basis, consider adding gentle to moderate exercises to your routine. Doing daily stretches or simply getting out and walking a few times a week can give you an excellent boost. If you currently have an exercise routine, keep it up! And the old tradition of the family after-dinner walk is worth reviving for health reasons as well as for the sense of connectedness it offers.

Managing Demands at Work or School

Work-related or school-related stress can interfere with even the most well conceived attempts at behavioral change. Such stress might result from heavy workloads, demanding deadlines, burdensome responsibilities, difficulties with coworkers, or other kinds of troubling circumstances that may arise. Such circumstances can impact many other activities, including interfering with your ComB practice. But even if you have a challenging job or a busy academic life, perhaps work pressures can be modified, at least temporarily, so you are able to work on your BFRB problem. At the very least, resist the temptation to volunteer for additional work. In addition, see if you may be allowed to share or delegate some responsibilities. Speak up and ask for help whenever possible. If these options are unrealistic in your situation, try brainstorming other ideas with a friend, coworker, or family member. Even if there are no apparent solutions to work or school problems, many of our clients have found that the structure and discipline associated with their efforts to stop pulling or picking have actually had the unexpected benefit of helping them be more efficient and more focused on school and work demands. Perhaps that will be true for you as well.

Factoring in Family Obligations and Interpersonal Commitments

Another common challenge is ongoing obligations involving one's family. Children demand a great deal of time, attention, and emotional energy; older relatives may also require your time, effort, and support due to health or other problems. In either case, it can be difficult to focus on your own needs. And if you are a member of the "sandwich" generation—managing the needs of both your aging parents and your children—the demands can derail even the most carefully conceived plan to attend to your own needs.

How can you handle obligations such as these and at the same time realistically add your recovery program to the mix? One possibility is to find others to share the burden. If you are a parent, having the expectation that your children will assist with some household chores not only helps you, it also helps enhance their own sense of responsibility and potentially their competence, confidence, and self-esteem. In addition, you might join or set up a carpooling arrangement with some other parents, a babysitting coop, or, if it is within your means, you might hire someone to take over some household chores. Asking your spouse or partner to help lighten your load may be worth a try. Maybe none of these suggestions is at all practical in your circumstances, or maybe your life has other demands that are not even addressed here. If that is the case, then the next section may be especially important for you as you move forward.

The Importance of Self-Care

When you are tired, stressed, or lacking in physical or emotional energy, it may be impossible to function at your best, even under ordinary circumstances. And the challenge is even greater if you are trying to make a major life change such as recovering from your BFRB, because when you don't feel healthy and strong, self-care may fall to the bottom of your "To Do" list. So try to think of tending to your health as a way to reduce your level of stress in the long run. Engaging in a variety of health-promoting activities will help you feel better physically, mentally, and emotionally, and will improve your ability to manage things. Simultaneously, you will experience the strong, positive message that your well-being is important! This does not have to involve an abrupt and dramatic change in your lifestyle; even small changes in your day-to-day life can yield big results over time by decreasing your stress and increasing your focus, motivation, and energy level.

You can start anywhere—eating healthier, getting more exercise, spending more time in the natural world, decreasing time on "screens," or getting more sleep are just a few examples. For instance, if you have a habit of not getting enough sleep, you may feel chronically tired, irritable, and unproductive. In these states you may be more likely to give in to picking and pulling, and less likely to be able to stick to your ComB program. Telling yourself to just get more sleep is usually easier said than done. Still, if you can help yourself in this way, you won't be sorry. We recommend that you start out with some minor modifications in your daily routine. Try turning off your TV or computer earlier in the evening and go to bed fifteen minutes earlier for a few nights. When you have accomplished that, go to bed another fifteen minutes earlier—and so on—until you have a bedtime schedule that allows for a more satisfying night's sleep. Be sure to plan your evening's activities so they fit into your adjusted bedtime schedules.

MAKING THE LEAP

If you feel unsure about whether you are ready to tackle your BFRB, don't lose heart: Keep reading this book, for doing so will help you learn much more about your problem and how ComB can help you solve it. Many people say that knowledge is power. If so, reading this book will provide you with some of the power you will need to take the next step—when the time is right for you.

But if you *do* feel ready to change your life for the better, and if you *do* feel ready to tackle the obstacles that might get in your way, read on with a "take action" attitude. Tell yourself that there's no time like the present to begin the process of healing, and trust that the book you are holding in your hand can guide you on your path. So, ready or not, go ahead to the next chapter to find out how to start taking charge.

CHAPTER 3

Ready, Set, Go!

In this chapter we will provide an overview of the ComB program, from beginning to end, introduce you to the five "SCAMP" domains (Sensory, Cognitive, Affective, Motor, and Place), and show you how factors within each domain contribute to your BFRB. We want you to begin to think about the elements within each domain that are most relevant to your problem. In this chapter you will be introduced to methods that will keep these elements from triggering picking or pulling episodes by creating and employing an individualized plan tailored to your unique picking or pulling profile. The ComB model will be your essential guide as you move through the process of recovery, and SCAMP will help you organize your plan.

COMB AND SCAMP

As a reminder, ComB stands for the "Comprehensive Behavioral Approach." The "Com" refers to the word "comprehensive," which means that this approach considers a wide range of factors and features—those "essential ingredients" that constitute important elements in problems associated with your hair pulling and skin picking. The "B" in ComB refers to the "behavioral" approach to understanding the various aspects of BFRBs, and the nature of the behavioral and cognitive techniques designed to address these problems. As you will see, the specific combination of the various elements in the ComB approach is unique to you, so only ones that seem most applicable will become part of your program.

The SCAMP acronym, which will be covered in this chapter and in later chapters, is the lynchpin of the ComB approach. It facilitates the quick recall of five major domains, clusters of variables that are implicated in BFRBs. While the word "scamp" is a pure convenience, it suggests an amusing but mischievous child. It may be that an attitude characterized by playfulness and a sense of humor will help you in your efforts ahead. Within each of these domains are specific elements that constitute your unique hair pulling or skin picking pattern, your "profile." Throughout the rest of this book, SCAMP will help you identify domains that trigger and maintain your picking or pulling episodes and the particular elements within each domain that can be targeted for change. As you read each chapter you will have the opportunity to identify specific interventions that you might want to consider as facilitators of change. This information will guide you in developing your individualized program—one that can positively impact and, we hope, ultimately vanquish your BFRB and allow you to achieve a happier and healthier life.

THE COMB PROGRAM, STEP BY STEP

Your ComB program may seem challenging, but it may help you to know that it involves only three basic stages, and that in each stage you will increase your knowledge and skills and will move further along toward recovery. Each chapter in this book will provide you with valuable information. By moving through the stages, you will be well on the way to reaching your goal. Here is a sneak preview.

Stage 1: Building Your Awareness. In this stage, you will identify the triggers and consequences of engaging in BFRBs that instigate and maintain your hair pulling or skin picking.

Stage 2: Planning and Preparation. Here, you will identify and prepare to use promising interventions to address the triggers and consequences you have identified in Stage 1.

Stage 3: Putting Your Plan into Action. In this final stage, you will introduce the interventions you have chosen into your daily routine, and you will make changes in your plan as your circumstances require.

Within each stage, you will have corresponding forms to work with to help you successfully complete each step of the program. All of these forms can be found on the New Harbinger website: www.newharbinger .com/43645. Sample small versions of the forms can be found in the Appendix of this book, but please go to the online site to print out larger copies that will be more convenient for you to actually fill in.

Stage 1: *Self-Monitoring Form.* This form will help you attend to and record important details involved in your BFRB so that you can effectively address them.

Stage 2: *Master List of Interventions.* Here are many ideas for interventions within each SCAMP domain. This list will help you choose healthy alternatives to address needs previously met through pulling and picking.

Stage 3: *Action Plan.* This form will help you organize your interventions as you put your plan into practice, and will guide you in making necessary modifications to your plan as you gain experience and feedback from your efforts.

We encourage you to familiarize yourself with these three important forms. At this time, however, focus on the *Self-Monitoring Form*, as you are now ready to begin Stage 1 of your program. Here is some additional guidance as you begin this crucial stage, which sets the foundation for the remaining stages of your program.

Stage 1: Building Your Awareness

In developing your plan, you will need to become aware of many details of your picking or pulling, and we strongly suggest that you use your *Self-Monitoring Forms* for this purpose. If knowledge is power, learning as much as you can about your BFRB will maximize your chances of success. If you are like most people, you will probably find it somewhat burdensome to document the details of BFRB episodes. But even if you were aware of most of the details about an episode while it was happening, you will probably find that it is impossible to recall all of the details at a later time. So, while we know that it might be a chore to record the detailed information about an episode as soon as possible, please don't skip this step. The *Self-Monitoring Forms* will help you gather the information that you will need as you move forward with your program, and help you organize it in a logical and useful way. Please use the forms that you have printed out to help you document at least three episodes—perhaps two on typical weekdays and one on a typical weekend day.

After you have documented those episodes, you can ask yourself this question: "What did I learn from this experience?" It is likely that you discovered some details or patterns of behavior that had previously been hidden because they had been so much a part of your daily routine. But when exposed through raised awareness, these details and behavioral patterns will become more obvious and predictable—and therefore potentially more manageable. It is hard to change patterns of behavior unless you are fully aware of them.

As you read through the rest of this book, you will have many opportunities to practice working on the *Self-Monitoring Forms*, as well as the other forms, and soon you should be very comfortable completing all of them. For now, just focus on this one. Remember that your plan will flow from the information you gather on it, and that it will be dynamic and individualized. Throughout the process of working with the ComB method, try to maintain an attitude of curiosity, patience, and self-acceptance as you take steps toward self-improvement.

> **TRY IT!** Document three episodes (include at least two week-days and one weekend day) on three Self-Monitoring Forms. The forms don't have to look pretty or be perfect. Stick with it—we strongly believe that your efforts will be rewarded! After doing this exercise, write down what you learned in the comments section of each form.

Note that the next five chapters will be devoted to describing each SCAMP domain in great detail, so that you will become even more acutely aware of elements within your Sensory, Cognitive, Affective, Motor, and Place domains by focusing on each one separately.

Now let's preview what will come in the second and third phases of your program.

Stage 2: Planning and Preparation

The next step will be to use the information from your completed *Self-Monitoring Forms* to identify potential interventions that are appropriate for your program. As you may already be aware, the acronym SCAMP has two functions: The first is to help you organize the circumstances and experiences that trigger and maintain your picking or pulling into their relevant domains. The second function is to help you identify potentially helpful interventions that address those specific elements within those domains. This is why observing and documenting your picking or pulling using the *Self-Monitoring Forms* is so important: Your use of those forms will guide you through the process, and help you gather important and useful information.

In the five chapters that follow in part 2 of this book, you will find detailed descriptions of each of the five SCAMP domains that typically contribute to hair pulling and skin picking. You will also learn how to use interventions that are specific to each domain and geared to your individual needs. Here is a brief glimpse at the kinds of interventions within each SCAMP domain that you will be learning more about in part 2:

Sensory: In this domain, you will focus on finding substitutes and activities that divert you from picking and pulling by stimulating or soothing your senses.

Cognitive: Here, you will be encouraged to challenge thoughts and beliefs that encourage you to pick or pull. You will learn to replace or counter them with more realistic and helpful "words of wisdom."

Affective: Within this domain, you will be encouraged to discover and employ healthy methods of managing your emotions and other uncomfortable feelings, instead of picking or pulling.

Motor: Here, you will focus on identifying and addressing any unconscious habits, movements, and body positions that encourage your picking and pulling. You will increase your awareness through the use of barriers, for example, that impede or prevent contact between your hands and hair or skin, and by providing alternative ways to keep your hands busy and away from your picking and pulling sites.

Place: The place domain includes all aspects of your environment or setting (for instance, time of day, situation, or objects within your physical environment) that set the stage for picking and pulling. The interventions that will be described will serve to eliminate or decrease the power of these cues, thereby making those environments less "BFRB friendly."

Stage 3: Putting Your Plan into Action

Using the information gathered from your *Self-Monitoring Forms* and the interventions you have chosen to employ from the *Master*

List of Interventions, you will be ready to put your plan into action! The interventions should be organized and ready to use. The *Action Plan* forms will enable you to write down where, when, and how you plan to use your interventions. They also enable you to monitor the effectiveness of your interventions. Weekly use of these forms will help guide you through modification of your program to gain increasing mastery over your BFRB.

ONE PERSON'S JOURNEY

Your story is unique, but you may have more in common with other people with BFRBs than you think. Therefore, throughout this book, we will be offering examples that represent different variations within BFRBs, as well as some common threads. We will now follow one person as she goes through her process of recovery. Her story, as described here, will take you beyond the first stage of her program and provide you with a foreshadowing of program elements to be found in the later stages.

Alicia's Story

Alicia is forty years old and has been pulling hair from her scalp since she was eleven. The pulling has waxed and waned in severity over the years. Currently her hair is thinned out all over her scalp and she has a few silver dollar-sized bald areas above her ears. She is very worried because it is getting harder and harder for her to cover up her hair loss. She is a member of the TLC Foundation, where she read about the ComB method and decided to try it. During the first stage of the program she identified details of her episodes and documented them on Self-Monitoring Forms. Living with her pulling problem for so long made her doubt that there was any more to learn about it, so she considered skipping the self-monitoring phase. But "just to be safe," Alicia decided that she would do self-monitoring for three days, as recommended. She placed some copies of the form in her purse so that she could document her pulling episodes whether she was at home, driving, or in the office. Here we will focus only on her efforts to address her hair pulling that occurred while she commuted to work.

Just being attentive to her hair pulling had a positive effect. While she was driving to work on a summer day she was stuck in especially slow-moving traffic. While that was stressful enough, on top of that she had been deep in thought about the demanding workload that faced her at the office. After sitting in rush hour traffic for almost a half hour, she caught herself flicking a hair out of the open car window. Now touching her scalp she could feel that one bald spot felt extra tender and seemed bigger than before. She knew now that she had been pulling out a number of hairs without even realizing it. Just touching the bald spot, she noticed, made her want to pull more, but she forced herself to grip the wheel tightly with both hands. As soon as she got to work, she documented what happened.

Stage 1: Building Her Awareness

Here is what Alicia wrote on her *Self-Monitoring Form* that morning after her commute to work. Although we have highlighted the domains, you do not have to do so at this point. By the time you get through later chapters, it will be easy for you to do that.

Self-Monitoring Form
Where and What: In car, driving to work.
When: Tues, Feb. 3, morning
I realized that I had flicked a hair out the window after I had been sitting in rush-hour traffic. Then I touched my scalp and felt that my bald spot was bigger than before. I thought I would know when I pulled, but sometimes this habit is automatic.   S (C) A (M) P

I was stressed because of traffic and worried about a work assignment.	S C (A) M P
Sitting, left elbow bent on armrest, head resting on my left hand. Other hand on steering wheel.	S C A (M) (P)
In the car, by myself, early morning going to work.	S C A M (P)

What I did with the "product": I tossed it.

First aware of urge/behavior (0-4): 3	Amount that I picked or pulled (0-4): 3
0 = Entering situation, 4 = Mid to late in episode	0 = None, 4 = Extreme

Comments: So much that I was not aware of what led to my pulling!

An important thing that Alicia noticed when she filled out the *Self-Monitoring Form* was that she had been much less aware of her pulling behaviors than she had previously realized. She was also interested to see how the different domains contributed to her pulling—the car (Place), her unconscious pulling while seated with her elbow bent (Motor), while feeling stressed and tired (Affective), and thinking bothersome and unhelpful thoughts (Cognitive).

Alicia's *Self-Monitoring Form* gave her information she needed to begin to think about how to create her plan. Although she had been reluctant to use the form, she now saw that this first step would become the foundation on which a promising individualized treatment plan for her recovery could be built.

At this point Alicia realized that her prior efforts to overcome her HPD had failed because she had not had the information she had gained by doing self-monitoring. It was as if she had been "fighting with one hand behind her back." She decided to commit to the ComB process, hoping that the program would successfully guide her toward her goal.

Stage 2: Planning and Preparation

Based on what she had documented on her *Self-Monitoring Form,* Alicia identified some triggers and consequences that were maintaining her behavior. The circumstances that she identified were: her hand touching a tingling spot on her head and noticing sharp hairs; giving herself permission to pull sharp hairs; feeling stressed and tired; positioning herself with her elbow on the armrest; easily allowing her hand to reach her head; and noticing that the air in the car felt stuffy and uncomfortable. Then she looked at the *Master List of Interventions* and circled several ideas that she thought might be helpful.

Following that, Alicia put her plan into action by using the interventions written in her *Action Plan.* But before she could put her plan into action, she had to prepare by putting certain items she would use as interventions in the car.

Alicia prepared in the following way:

- She put a sticky note on the dashboard of her car that said, "Don't start or you won't be able to stop." She planned to read it out loud three times when she got in the car.

- She bought a small basket for intervention items and placed it within easy reach.

- She bought lightweight driving gloves and placed them in the basket.

- She placed a small, stiff-bristled brush in the basket.

- She placed her *Action Plan* form and a pen in the basket so she would remember to document her experiences.

Stage 3: Putting Her Plan into Action

Now Alicia was prepared to put her plan into action. All of the necessary supplies were available in the basket next to the driver's seat. Below is that part of her initial weekly plan for when she was driving her car, as she began her first week of employing interventions and documenting her use of each intervention.

Action Plan							
Situation (Location/Activity): Driving to work in the morning.							
When Started: Monday, Feb. 8, 8:15 a.m.							
Interventions (Circle Relevant Domain Letters)	S	M	T	W	T	F	S
Problem: Tingling on head. Intervention: Comb or brush hair or scratch head with back of pen. (S) C A M P	✓	✓ ✓		✓ ✓	✓		✓
Problem: Giving myself permission to pull. Intervention: Note on dashboard: "Once I start, I don't want to stop." Say out loud 3 times. S (C) A M (P)				✓		✓	✓
Problem: Hands close to head. Intervention: Wear gloves and grip steering wheel with both hands. S C A (M) P		✓	✓	✓			✓
Problem: Feeling stressed and tired. Intervention: Use deep breathing when stressed; crank up the air conditioner. S C (A) M P	✓	✓				✓	✓
Awareness (0-4) 0 = Entering setting 4 = Mid to late in episode	3	2	3	2	3	4	1
How much did I pick or pull? (0-4) 0 = None, 4 = Extreme	4	2	3	2	4	3	1
Comments: It seems like the gloves helped the most, but weren't enough all by themselves. I did like scratching my scalp with the handle of my comb, so I did that a fair amount and I think it really helped.							

Let's look at the information that Alicia gained from a week of self-recording. She documented her use of interventions, her levels of awareness, and ratings of how much she pulled. For one thing, Alicia saw that when she wore gloves, she did better than when she didn't—even when she used other interventions. You, like Alicia, will probably find some interventions more helpful than others. But remember that there is no one "silver bullet." For BFRBs it is rare for any one intervention to "do the trick"—that is, to work immediately and to remain effective as long as necessary for you to reach your goals. The more domains you address, the more likely it is that you will succeed by weakening more factors that keep your BFRB running and making it seem unstoppable. So, try to use a 3×3 approach: at least three interventions, from three domains at a time, with extra benefits if you do more!

GETTING READY TO MAKE SCAMP A PART OF YOUR LIFE

Each chapter in part 2 of this book, explores one of the SCAMP domains, and will give you practice in using the appropriate forms. As you read them, you may choose to add interventions from each SCAMP chapter that you complete. By the time you get to chapter 9 ("Putting It All Together"), you will appreciate more the importance of each domain and how elements from within it impact your picking or pulling. Along the way, you may have noted many potential interventions from the five domains, some of which you might employ in your program. You might also add or discard previous ideas as you learn what works best for you. As you modify your program, try to use our suggested the 3×3 formula.

If you want to "test drive" your initial plan before you get to chapter 9, go ahead—you are likely to get a feel for this approach and to gain some useful experience in the process. But be aware that it is the *combination of interventions from all of your relevant domains that will give you the best chance for a full recovery.* The information that you will gain from reading all of the chapters in part 2 of this book will help you decide on the interventions from each domain that fit your unique profile.

After choosing interventions for all the settings in which your BFRB occurs, you might think that all you have to do is to follow the plan and document your progress. But your recovery will be a dynamic and nuanced process, so don't expect to have a perfect plan or overwhelming results early on. This is a work in progress, and you can and should modify your plan to suit your needs and circumstances over time.

Be aware that as you go through the rest of this book you may notice that, before you were introduced to ComB, you had previously tried a number of the recommended interventions (such as wearing a hat, or putting bandages on your fingers) and you may have gotten discouraged when they didn't work. By themselves, and without being part of a broader, cohesive plan, each alone wasn't powerful enough to override your urges or habitual behavior routines. Also, they likely didn't address certain elements within other domains that operated to keep your BFRB alive and well. Those same interventions, however, can be very useful when operating within a broader range of interventions that weaken the BFRB on several fronts.

Other than getting started on your *Self-Monitoring Forms*, you don't have to complete any more forms at this time! You still have quite a bit to learn, so you don't need to rush. By the time you get to chapter 9 you will be much better informed than you are at this point, and will have had time to think about and try out a variety of interventions that together will greatly increase your ability to reach your goal.

CULTIVATE A PATIENT AND PERSISTENT ATTITUDE

Think of this process as one of exploration and experimentation, so try to be patient, persistent, and honest with yourself as you move forward. If you are not progressing in a satisfying way, this probably means that you have not yet identified and implemented the best "formula" for your recovery. Plan to make a number of revisions as you refine your plan, or as your circumstances change. As you try out different combinations of interventions, take note when a particular intervention is not as helpful as you had hoped. If you try an intervention a few times and it doesn't help, go ahead and substitute different ones, or a different combination, until you find a more effective plan. If you try an intervention and it seems to make things worse, abandon it and move on.

QUICK REVIEW

You now have an overview of the process by which you can achieve your goal:

- Increase your awareness by using your *Self-Monitoring Forms* in selected settings.

- Familiarize yourself with the *Action Plan* and the *Master List of Interventions* that you will use in later stages of your program.

- Begin to envision a possible *Action Plan* for at least one location, based on you current understanding of how ComB works.

Cultivate creative problem-solving, patience, and persistence—they will serve you well! Even in the long run, this will be a work in progress and in flux; don't expect to create a perfect plan that will carry you through your entire recovery effort and beyond. Over time, your needs will change, so your plan will need to change as well. This is to be expected; change is inevitable in life, so be prepared to adapt to your evolving circumstances and needs.

If you are feeling a bit overwhelmed at this point, don't fret. You have had your BFRB for months—or more likely, for years. This is a healing process that may seem complex and challenging, but be reassured that we will guide you well. Just take it step by step and recognize that you are already on the right path—after all, you have already gotten to this point in this book. Let the healing begin!

PART 2

SCAMP:
The Five Domains
of Body-Focused
Repetitive Behaviors

CHAPTER 4

The Sensory Domain

Take a moment to consider your major senses: sight, hearing, touch, smell, and taste enable you to enjoy some of your most important sources of pleasure. Without them you couldn't experience fully a beautiful sunset, a great concert, the soft texture of a baby's cheek, the sweet aroma of a rose, or the taste of hot apple pie. But our senses can also get us into trouble, and because they often play a large role in picking and pulling problems it is fitting that "S," which represents the Sensory domain, will be the first SCAMP letter that we will explore.

GROOMING: IT'S NATURAL!

Many animals instinctively engage in grooming, and we humans are no exception. Grooming serves to keep the body's protective "envelope"—the skin, scalp, hair, nails, and cuticles—healthy by keeping it intact, clean, smooth, and free from nuisances such as insects, thorns, or debris that might cling to it. Our tactile and visual systems are key parts of this defense system. Our skin is endowed with millions of nerve cells, which allow us to sense potential problems on the body's surface that might cause us harm. Our sense of vision allows us to see potential problems that require our attention. Together, these two senses signal our brain to take action when necessary.

Grooming has psychological and social aspects, too. Since hair, skin, and nails are important aspects of our appearance, being well groomed or engaging in self-grooming can have a positive impact on our relationships, on our sense of self, and our health, as well. It is no surprise, then, that self-grooming is a natural impulse, with most of us engaging in it on a daily basis. We cleanse and moisturize our face and body; smooth jagged skin; cut, clip, and file our nails; and perhaps squeeze pimples or scratch off scabs. Grooming also involves brushing, washing, and styling our hair, as well as shaving or using scissors or tweezers to remove hairs that are stray, gray, or otherwise unwanted. In fact, these activities are so much a part of life, that people who do not engage in adequate grooming can be thought of as off-putting, dirty, odd, and to be avoided if possible.

Normal, healthy grooming ordinarily stays within certain boundaries. It is true that at one time or another most of us have gotten carried away and may have done some damage to our skin, hair, scalp, cuticles, or nails in our grooming efforts. But when we go too far and cause significant cosmetic problems or physical damage over an extended period of time—as is the case with BFRB disorders—the blessing of the senses can feel like a curse.

THE SENSORY ASPECTS OF BFRBS

Sensations serve many purposes and are often signals from within our body that lead to actions. Many of these actions are direct efforts to reduce discomfort, while others are attempts to achieve pleasurable sensations, Patterns of hair pulling and skin picking typically involve a vicious cycle set into motion by certain sensations and the effect they have on other domains, such as emotional reactions (Affective domain) to those sensations and beliefs (Cognitive domain) about how those sensations should be addressed.

Pain, Pleasure, or Both?

If you are like most people in your situation, your natural grooming tendencies have gotten out of control for a variety of reasons, and a number of sensory elements contribute to your picking or pulling. Many of these represent an effort to relieve distress by eliminating imperfections that are seen or felt, the desire to have certain sensory experiences that are pleasurable or interesting, or in many cases a combination of both.

Sensory triggers that often precipitate hair pulling include hairs that create visual or tactile discomfort. In the majority of cases, the person's eyes and hands work together. However, it is not unusual for one or the other to be the primary "driver" of the process.

If you pull your hair, the triggers may include the imperfect appearance or texture of your eyelashes, eyebrows, scalp hairs, pubic hairs, or hair on your arms or legs. Specific hairs may look or feel as if they are the wrong color, the wrong texture, too long, too thin, too thick, too curly, too straight, or may have split ends. Some people report that the problem isn't the hair itself, but that it is in the wrong place, is out of line, or lacks symmetry.

If you are a skin picker, you may be bothered by unwanted imperfections on your face, back, chest, feet, arms, legs, cuticles, or other areas on your body. Visual cues may include seeing redness or other discoloration; tactile irritants include scabs, bumps, or skin that is rough, painful, itchy, flaky, or dry. Acne can be especially problematic because of the visibility of pimples on the face and sensations of pressure or soreness. Even in the case of "out of sight" areas such as the chest, shoulders, or back, many people experience great satisfaction and relief when they are able to successfully smooth out their skin. You may find it rewarding when you are able to remove these imperfections, smooth the skin, pop a pimple, or remove a scab. At these moments, it is easy to forget that in most cases your efforts do not turn out as well as you might have wished.

Instead of, or in addition to, the effort to get rid of hair or skin that looks or feels unappealing, maybe your goal is to receive a desirable sensation, perhaps a pleasurable feeling when a hair is extracted, or a unique sensation that you experience as desirable when scabs are removed or a pimple is popped. Or perhaps the main sensory payoff for you is the satisfaction you experience *after* the extraction, when you pull a hair that has a plump or moist root, or one that has an interesting shaft that you enjoy examining, playing with, touching to your lips, splitting the shaft, picking or biting off the follicle, or even swallowing the root or the hair itself. If you pick at your skin, perhaps the bit of skin or a skin "product" (pus, scab, etc.) is fascinating to touch or look at or taste, or you might enjoy the sensation of peeling away a layer of skin and manipulating it with your fingers. If any of these activities seem bizarre or repulsive to you, it is because you do not enjoy them. The fact that others do, reminds us of the wide range of activities that are within the potential for human beings to enjoy.

WHEN ONE THING LEADS TO ANOTHER: THE SEQUENCE OF PICKING OR PULLING EPISODES

In addition to predictable BFRB sensory elements of visual or tactile experiences, there is also a predictable sequence (or chain) of behaviors that are an integral part of a person's routine. In these, sensations are involved in each link in the chain: (1) pre-BFRB behaviors, such as exposing, touching, and searching for possible targets; (2) performance of the BFRB, such as the actual removal of hair or picking, scratching, or squeezing of the skin; and (3) disposition of the pulled hairs or removed fragments of skin, in other words, what is done with the products derived from picking, pulling, and related behaviors. In the example below you will see how one step leads to the next, and how easy it is to slide down the slippery slope of a BFRB episode.

Sensory experiences that can trigger the initial phase of your picking or pulling episodes. Certain subtle sensations can create impulses to search for, touch, or visually examine particular hairs or areas of the skin. These initial actions, whether they are conscious or unconscious, are capable of setting the sequence in motion. Although the senses of hearing, smell, or taste are sometimes involved, for most people touch and vision are the most prominent senses. An early step in your picking or pulling routine may involve a movement of your hand toward the "target" area in response to localized sensations of itch, pain, tingling, burning, or others. Perhaps you are consciously aware of the sensation and purposely respond to it. Alternatively, your hand may move to the target area automatically and therefore outside of your awareness. (We will focus on automatic movements in a later chapter.) In either case, once contact has occurred, the fingertips can, with or without awareness, search for and detect potential targets. Certain features of your hair or skin are perhaps bothersome or may otherwise be of some particular interest to you. If so, these features stimulate your impulse to touch, search, isolate the targeted hair or bit of skin, and then to take further action. Simultaneously, the tactile sensations that you experience as you press, rub, or otherwise stimulate the nerve cells of the skin, cuticles, or scalp can further propel the process along to the next step in the sequence.

The other major contributor during this early stage is visual perception. When vision is involved it usually is associated with a more conscious awareness of BFRB activities. For instance, you might notice a bump, scab, or other "flaw" on your arm or leg when you are changing your clothes. There are other times that your skin is exposed and possibly under your scrutiny, such as when you are using the toilet, getting ready to take a shower, or washing your face. Visual cues are enhanced by brightly lit mirrors and magnifying mirrors that can reveal even minor flaws that most people wouldn't ordinarily notice, such as asymmetry or unevenness in the hairline, or variations in hair color or texture on the scalp, eyebrows, or eyelashes. A man might notice a flaw on his face when shaving, while a woman may be especially vulnerable when applying or removing makeup.

The interplay between visual and tactile stimuli can create a powerful "feedback loop." See if this scenario contains any familiar elements: With your fingers you detect an annoying imperfection on your skin or you detect a "target hair" that seems ripe for the pulling. Your fingers get busy investigating it, and sensations at the site and feelings on the fingertips lead to strong urges to take action. You go to a private place, such as a bathroom or bedroom, or take out a mirror that you keep close by so you can examine it more closely. Maybe you seek out a brightly lit place to allow you to scrutinize the area of interest more closely. After a preliminary examination, you might continue to stroke, rub, visually examine, or otherwise explore your skin or scalp, searching for or isolating a specific hair or area of the skin in preparation for the next step. You might lean toward a mirror and grab tweezers or other implements to gain better access the specific hair or blemish.

Sensations during active picking or pulling and removal efforts. The moment when hairs are extracted or areas of the skin are picked at can be the source of the most powerful sensations in the BFRB sequence. The primary sensation at that moment is often tactile, although the visual system may be an important sensory component as well, as noted above.

You may experience a variety of pleasurable or interesting sensations as the hair is extracted. For some individuals with sensitive hearing, the sound of a quiet "pop" can also be gratifying. If you engage in skin picking or trying to extract ingrown hairs, most likely you visually home in on your targets, while you squeeze, pick at, scratch, or otherwise excoriate the skin in order to remove rough or irregular spots that you have identified by sight or touch. Pimples or acne can present their own special challenges because of their physical discomfort and unattractive appearance. Individuals are often prone to squeeze pimples in hopes that they will heal faster, even when they know that they aren't ready to be "popped" and that the action is thus likely to do more harm than good. These activities can involve the use of magnifying glasses, mirrors, and enhanced lighting for increased visual acuity, and tweezers, needles, or pins to facilitate the process.

Post-picking and post-pulling activities. What do you do, if anything, with the hair or bit of skin after it's removed? Perhaps you look at or manipulate the extracted hair or skin-related "product." Or you may scrutinize the pulling or picking site to assess the outcome of your efforts. In fact, for some individuals, the aftermath of the pulling or picking, rather than the activity itself, may provide the most powerful sensory payoff. Positive post-pulling experiences might include securing and examining hair shafts with large, waxy, or blood-tipped roots. Other common post-pulling sensory "payoffs" commonly involve playing with or otherwise manipulating an extracted hair—twisting it, or touching the cool, moist root to sensitive skin on the face, lips, or hand. Oral activities are often involved as well, with people drawing the hair between their lips or teeth, chewing on a shaft of the hair, biting off the hair bulb, or swallowing the root or the hair itself. If you pick at your skin you may likely examine the pus, scab, or bit of skin that has been removed after popping a pimple, pulling off a scab, or scratching at a bump. Another common post-picking behavior is to roll or knead a scab or fragment of skin between the fingers or fingernails for tactile stimulation. As is the case with hair pulling, oral activities are common as well. These activities might include biting, chewing, or ingesting the scab or bits of dry skin.

BFRB'S VICIOUS CYCLE

One of the most frustrating aspects of BFRBs is that picking or pulling produces additional sensory experiences that can lead to further picking or pulling, thereby fueling the recurring cycle of harmful behavior. This frequently occurs in the form of repeated "mini-sequences" within a given picking or pulling episode. For instance, when pulling one hair or picking at one scab or bump feels really satisfying, it might well lead you to move on to a nearby target, which in turn leads to more picking or pulling. Alternatively, if you do not achieve your goal of successfully removing the target hair (for example, the "wrong" hair was pulled) or a satisfying outcome when addressing a skin blemish (for example, the pimple didn't "pop") on the first try, you are very likely to continue pulling or picking in efforts to achieve your goal.

This cycle creates both short-term and long-term problems. Perhaps you prematurely remove scabs or otherwise try to "improve" previously damaged skin. This can cause your skin to become raw, rough, or swollen, which can increase your tendency to pick at those areas, thereby causing more pain, bleeding, or irritated, raw, rough skin. In the case of hair pulling, injury to the scalp or the annoying feel of prickly regrowth generates new and uncomfortable sensations that serve to trigger further activity. Most people are likely to get discouraged when, day after day, they see and feel the damage that they have done. They might just give up and accept their BFRB as inevitable. Some will get drawn into becoming accustomed to and even encouraging some unique aspect of their condition—for instance, when bald spots are present and hairs begin to grow within the bare area, or if the area does not have a clean boundary, they will pull additional hairs in efforts to maintain a satisfyingly smooth surface or perimeter. In this way, the bald spot is maintained and usually grows larger and larger. A similar thing happens with skin picking when attention to blemishes and imperfections moves to healthy and intact skin.

In these ways BFRBs hijack what started out as ordinary grooming, causing picking or pulling to expand into episodes of increasingly uncontrolled behavior. The resulting damage produces even more sensations that provoke further picking or pulling and the BFRBs becomes harder and harder to manage.

WHY IS IT SO HARD TO STOP?

The hold your BFRB has on you can be compelling when it involves a determination to achieve desirable sensations or outcomes. In some ways it can be similar to gambling or the challenge of a treasure hunt, such as, "Will I (finally) get a hair with a 'good' root that I can nibble on?" or "Can I get rid of that annoying scab without causing a lot of bleeding?" Because you likely have achieved your goal some of the time, the risk may seem worth taking, even though deep down you might know that there is a good chance that you will just make things worse.

In addition, an almost universal result of BFRBs is that more imperfections are created than removed, and these, in all likelihood, will become future BFRB targets. For instance, trying to "improve" your appearance by prematurely removing scabs or squeezing pimples can create damaged areas that become raw, rough, or swollen, thereby creating additional targets. The sharp tips or awkward angles of emerging hairs that are growing in to replace previously pulled ones can likewise lead to further damage.

Ironically, if the desire to eliminate unpleasant sensations or to achieve desirable ones may have led you start picking or pulling, you may very well end up creating damage that further drives your BFRB. Even when episodes give you immediate relief from unwanted sensations, these can be followed by longer term medical issues, including physical pain, bleeding, open wounds, baldness, infections, scarring, and disfigurement. But unfortunately, even in the face of these common negative results, it can be extremely hard to stop, since, as you may already realize, the immediate desirable effects of pulling and picking tend to have a more powerful impact on your behavior patterns than the negative, delayed ones do. Over time, as the problem gets worse, you—along with others who struggle with BFRBs—may find yourself even more compelled to repeat the experience over and over again. You may hope against hope that you can be successful in achieving or reexperiencing the rewards of picking or pulling and that your SPD or HPD will resolve itself. Instead, the problem grows stronger and more out of control. This is why so many people who start out with simple efforts to address a minor problem with skin or hair, or who find that these activities can produce desirable sensations, are so dismayed to find that their behavior has morphed into a full-fledged and chronic disorder, challenging to overcome and with the potential of spoiling one's life.

MANAGING THE SENSORY ASPECTS OF YOUR BFRB

The sensory cues that lead to picking or pulling can be addressed by decreasing visual or tactile triggers and by engaging in activities that can meet your body's sensory needs in healthier ways.

Prevention Through Healthy Grooming

There is an old saying that an ounce of prevention is worth a pound of cure, and nowhere is this truer than in the case of BFRBs. Many of the conditions that trigger and maintain picking and pulling can be prevented through healthy skin and hair care. If you pick at your skin, the frequent and regular use of skin products such as moisturizers, face masks, sunscreen, exfoliating pads and creams, oil and mineral bath supplies, and cuticle, hand, and foot care products can help you reduce or eliminate the dry, itchy, hard, or jagged skin that you target. Giving yourself a manicure or pedicure on a regular basis—carefully filing your nail with a gentle nail file, caring for your cuticles, and moisturizing your hands—will help keep your cuticles and nails healthy and provide beneficial self-care alternatives to skin picking. A warm bath with scented oils offers many sensory benefits that can help you relax, while a cool shower with a variety of exfoliating brushes and stimulating scented soaps can give you the sensory "jump start" that can get you up and out in the morning. There are many interesting books, magazine articles, and online videos available that can help you have beautiful and healthy skin, hands, and nails. We recommend that you explore the options and further educate yourself about how to take good care of your skin and nails in a healthy way.

If you pull your hair, make a commitment to use hair products that medicate, nourish, moisturize, and hydrate the hair and scalp as part of your regular routine. These can reduce scalp itching and the dry, brittle hairs that can serve as BFRB targets. In addition, gentle combing or brushing not only provides pleasurable stimulation to the scalp, but also distributes natural oils throughout your hair. That will also keep your hands busy. Getting your hair washed and cut on a regular basis, by a professional if that suits your circumstances, can provide pleasurable sensory input as well as keep hair free from split and dry ends.

When to Get Help

If ordinary grooming practices lead to increased scrutiny of your hair or skin, and thus put you at risk for picking or pulling, or if the damage is such that things aren't going to get better just by using healthy grooming techniques, you may need to access outside help. Perhaps you can put your nail care, eyebrow tweezing and shaping, hair cutting and coloring, or even aspects of your skin care in the hands of professionals, such as hair stylists or estheticians, for these services if your means allow. When stubborn hairs grow where they aren't wanted, or ingrown hairs are a problem, getting laser or electrolysis treatments can provide substantial benefits.

In more serious cases, it may be wise to go to a dermatologist for special products and procedures to address certain scalp or skin problems. There you can learn the most effective and medically sound way to treat acne or heal wounds. Seeking outside help in these ways, if you are able, may be just what you need to better handle significant sensory aspects involved in your BFRB.

If your budget doesn't allow for some of the services mentioned above, you might be able to enlist the help of a trusted friend or family member for some of the simpler tasks, such as eyebrow grooming or manicures. But you may also decide that it is worth it to spend your holiday, birthday, vacation, or even "rainy day" money to get this kind of help. If you think about your situation as a medical condition, it might encourage you to proceed with useful treatments. Upon reflection, you may decide that the health and mental health costs of skin picking and hair pulling justify the costs of helpful, positive self-care activities.

Decrease Sensory Cues That Can Trigger BFRBs

Another way to reduce the power of sensory-related triggers is to decrease the visual or tactile cues that can trigger or maintain your BFRB.

Decrease tactile cues. This may involve minimizing contact between fingertips and potential target sites by blocking access to target areas. Try wearing clothes (including pajamas) that cover your arms, legs, and feet; or wear glasses that impede easy access to the eye area. Inexpensive plastic safety glasses can serve this purpose. Wearing gloves, bandages, or tape on your fingertips can help, too, by preventing easy access with your fingertips and hair or skin. Finally, certain hairstyles—such as some short cuts, or styles that involve pulling the hair back in a twist or pony tail—can discourage "playing" with the hair as they will keep the hair away from the face and impede easy grasping or teasing out individual strands of hair for pulling.

Reduce visual triggers. Visual cues that lead to picking or pulling can be minimized as well. For instance, dimming the lights in certain situations, like ones in which mirrors are present, can decrease your ability to detect and react to small flaws that are best left alone. Eliminating unnecessary mirrors by removing them or temporarily covering them can make a big difference, especially early in your recovery program. Our clients who try out interventions that decrease sensory triggers—such as covering mirrors or getting used to brushing their teeth, using the toilet, or taking a shower in low light—are often pleasantly surprised by how effective this simple change can be. You, too, may be pleased to find out that most bathroom activities do not require bright lights, and that it is quite helpful to be free from the temptation (tyranny?) of the mirrors in your bathroom or bedroom. Activities that do require a well-lit environment, such as putting on makeup, can be done in a different location, solely used for that purpose and therefore encountered less frequently.

Find healthy sources of sensory stimulation. It is often possible to stimulate your senses in alternative ways to stimulate or soothe the nervous system. It is important to honor your body's sensory needs, especially those that involve the fingertips and mouth area. You can try handling a variety of objects and "touch toys" that keep the hands busy and that are interesting to manipulate. Look for objects that are cold, sharp, smooth, soft, bendable, or that have other characteristics that meet your needs. One woman loved to find different kinds of stones and to keep them on hand to manipulate, and she especially enjoyed rubbing her finger against the ones with sharper edges. Other options might include the use of objects that feel smooth, velvety, metallic, puttylike, flexible, rough, or slippery—you name it—to manipulate with your fingertips or palms. Again, the important thing is to discover what meets your own sensory preferences, so feel free to experiment, innovate, and discover what is satisfying for you.

We have found that many people with BFRBs are creative individuals who have a strong sensitivity and responsiveness to aesthetics and the arts. If that describes you, honor that side of yourself. Certain hobbies or activities, such as gardening, cooking, baking, knitting, needlepoint, and jewelry making, are just a few examples of creative activities to keep your senses busy. If you like to do artwork, keep magic markers or colored pencils on hand to draw or doodle. Consider decorating your "trigger" locations (perhaps your office, study, bathroom, and bedroom) with items that give you visual pleasure, such as paintings, posters, or other artworks. These kinds of sensory experiences offer tactile and visual joys, as well as opportunities for engaging in productive and creative activities. They also serve as positive additions to an attractive environment and a healthy life.

Reduce auditory triggers. Irritating noises can grate on some people's nerves in ways that can fuel the fires of BFRBs, while too much silence can leave others feeling restless or bored. If this is true for you, consider surrounding yourself with music, nature recordings, or other types of auditory input that you find soothing, stimulating, or otherwise pleasurable. On a somewhat different "note," a number of our clients have reported that they enjoy singing, dancing, jogging, walking, or playing a musical instrument while alone, activities that provide varieties of sensory stimulation as well as other benefits. Come to think of it, how often do you pick or pull while you are dancing?

You may also benefit from stimulating the senses when you are involved in sedentary activities such as watching TV. Some people report that they really like the sound and feeling when they "pop" bubble wrap. It certainly doesn't hurt that this keeps the hands occupied as well. Others might find that this is the perfect time to put on hand lotion or polish their fingernails and toenails, activities that provide visual, tactile, and sometimes olfactory (smell) stimulation all at once, while keeping the hands busy.

Substitute oral sensory input. If your BFRB patterns activities involve the lips, mouth, or tongue, you can address your needs for oral stimulation by chewing gum, nibbling on the tips of pieces of raw spaghetti (it can substitute for hair bulbs), sucking on spicy, sour, or sweet hard candy or breath mints, or eating sunflower seeds. You can also use nonedibles such as dental floss, toothpicks, or gum stimulators. We recommend that you experiment with different objects and flavors to discover what interests you at different times of the day or while you are engaged in different activities. Everyone is different, so you can see that it is important to adopt a playful, experimental, and creative attitude so you can fully exploit the possibilities inherent in the domain of the senses.

Now that you have seen how powerful sensations can trigger and maintain your BFRB, you may wonder if it's too complicated a problem to solve. We want you to know that for the majority of individuals who make a sincere effort, this is *not* the case! As you read through this book you will be guided through the ComB three-stage method to create and implement a recovery program tailored to your individual needs.

To repeat, those stages are:

(1) **Building Your Awareness.** Here you will be monitoring and documenting your BFRB episodes, focusing on the Sensory domain. At this time you will use *Self-Monitoring Forms* in order to identify potential sensations that trigger a picking or pulling episode and identify the sensory outcomes that maintain the BFRB.

(2) **Planning and Preparation.** Here, aided by the *Master List of Interventions*, you will identify potentially useful interventions, gathering them and making them available in the places where they will be used.

(3) **Putting Your Plan into Action.** Here you will put your plan into action and record the effects of your plan for the week on the *Action Plan* form. Then, after one week of following your plan, modify it as needed.

(Reminder: These and all other forms can be found on the New Harbinger website: www.newharbinger.com/43645.)

We will illustrate this process by relating Monique's experiences and how she uses the information about sensory contributions to her hair pulling to choose and employ interventions to help her address her sensory issues.

Monique's Story

It is early evening and Monique is at home getting ready to meet some friends for drinks. As she decides what to wear, her hand travels to her head. Absent-mindedly, her fingers search her head for coarse hairs. When she finds one she grasps it between her thumb and forefinger. As a single hair is pulled out, she continues to explore the bumpy texture of each individual hair by rolling it between her fingers. Then she rubs the hair on her face and upper lip. Finally she discards the hair and her hand immediately goes back up to her head to search for another hair to pull. After twenty minutes have passed, she realizes that she still has not chosen an outfit for the evening. Moreover, she also realizes that she has created a small bald spot above her ear. At this point she goes into the bathroom to look into the mirror to inspect the damage. When examining more closely, Monique sees more course, dark hairs that seem out of place and that now bother her. She begins to remove them one by one, and repeats the same routine of rolling the hairs and rubbing them on her face and lip. Another thirty minutes pass and she has created more bald spots.

Monique suddenly "snaps out of it" and realizes that she was supposed to have joined her friends by now. She feels increasingly agitated as she tries brushing her hair to cover the damage, hoping that no one will notice. She finally gets out of the house, but worries that someone might ask about her bald spot.

Stage 1: Building Her Awareness

Here is how Monique later documented some of the sensory triggers during one of her picking episodes in her *Self-Monitoring Form*. Notice how the situation (location and activity) sets the stage.

Self-Monitoring Form					
Where and What: *Bathroom, getting ready to meet friends.*					
When: *Sat., Oct. 8*					
Felt coarse hairs on fingers.	S	C	A	M	P
Saw coarse hairs in mirror.	S	C	A	M	P
What I did with the "product": *Played with hair in between fingers, rubbed it on my face and lips.*	S	C	A	M	P

First aware of urge/behavior (0-4): *1*	Amount that I picked or pulled (0-4): *3*
0 = Entering situation, 4 = Mid to late in episode	0 = None, 4 = Extreme
Comments: *I like the way the hair feels in between my fingers, rubbing it on my face and tickling my upper lip.*	

In this example you can see how Monique was able to identify some of the tactile and visual sensations that were associated with her hair pulling. Interestingly, she realized that playing with the hair between her fingers and rubbing it on her lips were notable parts of her behavior pattern. She admitted to herself that she enjoyed these activities and knew that they encouraged her to pull again. She began to pay more attention to these aspects of her pulling, which in turn led her to the next step: finding potential interventions that could help her address them.

> **TRY IT!** Consider your most recent pulling or picking episode. Think about how sensory aspects might have affected you. If you find that this domain resonates for you, jot down some sensory experiences that either trigger your behavior or maintain it.

Stage 2: Planning and Preparation

Monique reviewed her *Self-Monitoring Form* and identified some sensory experiences that she now understood encouraged her hair pulling. She realized that sensory stimulation of her fingertips and lips would have to be addressed, as would her tendency to closely scrutinize her hair in the bathroom mirror.

She looked at the *Master List of Interventions* and circled the ones she thought would best help her address these sensory issues. Then she had some preparation to do:

She purchased an attractive nightlight and installed it, reasoning that it would provide enough light for most bathroom activities, but not for examining individual hairs.

She realized that using hairspray would make it less convenient to search for the usual target hairs, and the slight stickiness made it less likely that she would enjoy the feel of the hairs on her fingertips or on her lips.

She thought she might enjoy chewing gum while at home, so she bought a few packs.

She came up with the idea of wearing rubber bands on her wrists, as they would give her fingers something to fidget with.

> **TRY IT!** Now it's your turn. Using the *Master List of Interventions*, identify the sensory interventions that seem most appealing to you. Remember, the interventions should help satisfy some of your sensory needs, or provide other sensory input, so that you will not fall prey to pulling hair or picking skin.

Stage 3: Putting Her Plan into Action

Monique was now ready to use the information from earlier steps to create her plan and try it out. She did this for a week. Here is how it looked:

Action Plan							
Situation (Location/Activity): *Bathroom, washing up.*							
When Started: *Sun, Aug. 7*							
Interventions (Circle Relevant Domain Letters)	S	M	T	W	T	F	S

Problem: Free hands. Intervention: Fiddle with rubber bands. (S) C A M P	✓	✓			✓		✓
Problem: Playing with hair. Intervention: Wear hairspray daily. (S) C A M P		✓					✓
Problem: Looking closely in mirror. Intervention: Dim lights. (S) C A M P				✓	✓		
Problem: Rubbing hair on lip. Intervention: Chew gum. (S) C A M P				✓	✓		✓
Awareness (0-4) 0 = Entering setting 4 = Mid to late in episode	3	2	3	2	1	4	2
How much did I pick or pull? (0-4) 0 = None, 4 = Extreme	3	3	4	3	2	4	1
Comments: Used the regular light in my bathroom, put makeup kit in there, and my pulling was worse. Best day when I used all my interventions, worst day when I didn't use any of them.							

Monique saw the benefits of using interventions from the Sensory domain. Adding additional interventions from other domains would further round out her program.

This entire process will be described in detail in chapter 9 ("Putting It All Together"). At that point we will be asking you to put all of the stages of your own program together. For now, we want you to get familiar and comfortable with understanding each domain, one at a time, and to be in the position to evaluate the roles each plays in your BFRB. Then you will be able to construct an effective plan to undermine and weaken your BFRB and to eventually prevail.

You now have the first tool in your SCAMP toolbox! In this chapter you have learned about "S"—the Sensory domain of SCAMP—and how sensory interventions can offer healthy substitutes for picking or pulling, break the BFRB cycle, and help your skin and hair to grow healthy. In the next chapter you will learn about the "C" in SCAMP.

CHAPTER 5

The Cognitive Domain

In the previous chapter you learned about the role of the Sensory domain, the "S" in SCAMP. There you saw that certain *sensations* can trigger skin picking or hair pulling and are involved in maintaining these activities.

Now we will explore the "C" in SCAMP—the Cognitive domain, where other kinds of internal events may trigger your picking and pulling episodes. In this chapter you will learn how your ideas, thoughts, and beliefs—elements of the mind that the ComB approach clusters within the Cognitive domain—can play important roles in your problem. You may or may not already be aware that certain harmful thoughts and beliefs can encourage your picking or pulling. Here you will learn to challenge and replace those unhelpful thoughts with ones that will work for you in your efforts to gain control of your BFRB for good.

YOUR MIND: BEST FRIEND OR WORST ENEMY?

The human brain is unique in the animal kingdom. With its large, specialized cortex and language centers, your brain is involved in complex processes that, among many other things, shape your thoughts and beliefs for purposes of learning, planning, and relating to others on a day-to-day basis. These thoughts and beliefs are cognitions that, in turn, can interact with your emotions and behavior on a deep and powerful level.

Much of the time our thoughts are realistic enough, making sense of our experiences and helping us solve the problems we face. Thinking and reasoning can help us meet challenges in a constructive way. At other times, our thoughts are neutral, random, or inconsequential, floating through our mind without much impact. But there are also harmful cognitions that we all need to be aware of: inaccurate information and overly negative beliefs (and their opposites: denial or wishful thinking) that confuse and mislead us. For you and others with picking or pulling issues, misinformation or misguided assumptions or beliefs can contribute significantly to those problems. Identifying and correcting those misconceptions, then, can be a major part of the recovery process.

This chapter offers a detailed description of unhelpful thoughts and beliefs that may be triggering and maintaining your picking or pulling. It also includes suggestions that you can use to challenge and replace them with beliefs and thoughts that are realistic and helpful. This will require you to do some "thinking about your thinking." The skills involved in this process do not always come easily; in fact, the Cognitive domain can be the most subtle and elusive of the five domains. Don't let that discourage you, though; you will have help at every step of the way.

WHEN GROOMING GOES TOO FAR

Taking proper care of our physical appearance is undoubtedly good for our health and emotional well-being, and good for our relationships as well: You would probably agree that a daily routine of healthy grooming is important, including bathing, hair care, and skin care. And while we are at it, we can add trips to the beautician, hairdresser, hair-removal specialist, or barbershop to the list, if those are among your routine self-care practices, or are occasional additions to your routine. The degree we choose to indulge in any of the above activities requires a certain amount of self-discipline and good judgment, including knowing when enough is enough.

Much of our grooming is related to having healthy, attractive hair and skin. These are universally viewed as important symbols of youth, vitality, and beauty, and as such they carry more emotional meaning than many other human attributes.

Our ideas about our physical appearance, including the appearance of our hair and skin as well as what other parts of our body "should" look like, can affect our self-image as well as our sense of self-worth. Maintaining realistic standards about physical beauty in the face of all those beauty ads can be a challenge for all of us. In reality, despite our best intentions, most of us have taken our grooming activities too far on occasion.

In most cases, those overboard behaviors are short lived. But you and others who pick or pull may be especially sensitive to physical appearance for a number of reasons, including the influence of the media, with its preoccupation with the physical appearance of celebrities. Perhaps you, like so many others, have fallen prey to the overabundance of advertisements for cosmetics, hair care, skin care, and other beauty products that bombard us on a daily basis and that may have contributed to the development of unrealistic expectations about your appearance. For these and many other reasons, it may be harder for you than it is for most people to limit your hair or skin grooming practices so that you don't do more harm than good.

But misguided thoughts about attractiveness and health are only one concern within the Cognitive domain. Several others can also trip you up. As you work toward your recovery, your task regarding this domain will be to recognize them and to find effective ways to adjust your thoughts, attitudes, and beliefs about your hair and skin. The interventions in this chapter will help you "change your mind," which may well be one of the more important aspects of your recovery.

PROBLEM COGNITIONS AND INTERVENTIONS THAT CAN HELP

For the remainder of this chapter you will learn more about a number of cognitions that may be contributing to your picking or pulling difficulties and be guided in finding ways to successfully address them.

We can start by noting that there are different kinds of thoughts and beliefs that encourage picking and pulling. These include problematic thoughts about yourself, your BFRB, other people, and the healing process.

What follows are more details about these problematic cognitions. The good news is that there are ways to challenge them by using other words to more accurately describe the reality you are living, and then to access those new words when the BFRB part of your mind tries to *trick you*.

NOTE: For each of the misguided beliefs that follow, we have included an "intervention": some words of wisdom that we hope you will take to heart and act on, or a potential "Note to Self" statement for you to write down, memorize, and possibly recite or read aloud when you are in a setting where your BFRB typically shows up. There are many more in the *Short List of Interventions* in the Appendix of this book, and a whole lot more in the *Master List of Interventions* on the New Harbinger website. And—perhaps best of all—you may think up others for yourself.

Difficulty Tolerating Physical "Flaws"

Thoughts about grooming often reflect unrealistic standards about one's physical appearance. For instance, you may believe that minor skin or hair problems, or normal variations, such as asymmetries, are intolerable and need to be fixed, if at all possible. In reaction to those beliefs you might regularly engage in excessive efforts to try to eliminate these "unacceptable flaws," such as blemishes or unwanted hairs, asymmetries in your eyelashes, eyebrows, or hairline, or small irregularities of the skin.

Distorted or unrealistic thoughts about your physical appearance or grooming standards can be a driving force behind picking and pulling, since they can lead to the false belief that picking and pulling are "corrective" actions that must be taken, no matter what the price. As these effects accumulate, they too can become likely targets for further picking or pulling, in desperate and counterproductive efforts to correct the damage. Coming to terms about the reality of your attempts to improve your appearance will at least begin to chip away at your unhelpful beliefs.

Intervention: "I know I have gone too far when it looks worse than when I started (for example, bald areas, scabs, pain, bleeding, callouses, or unwanted changes in the texture or color of the hair). And if I have pain, infections, or scars, I know I am really in trouble!"

Believing That You Are Helpless

If you are like many people who pick or pull, you may at times be unaware that you have many distorted thoughts or false beliefs that trigger BFRB episodes. Without that awareness, you might think that your urges and episodes are random and unpredictable. It can be quite demoralizing to think that there is no rhyme or reason as to when your episodes happen. You might think that they come from out of the blue, or that there is nothing you can do to ward them off, because your "habit" is just too strong. Consequently, you may think that you will always be at the mercy of unpredictable urges, or that there is no way to escape from falling helplessly into a prolonged episode once you have begun to pull or pick.

Interventions: Given that it can be very challenging to get a handle on picking or pulling problems, it is easy to see why you might sometimes feel helpless and imagine that fighting your problem is a lost cause. But we are here to tell you that those beliefs are false! Cognitive interventions will give you healthy and realistic rebuttals that you can think about, write down, and practice saying or reading.

And remember this: On some level, you must hold out hope, or you would not be reading this book!

Minimizing or Ignoring the Problem

In contrast to the previous paragraph, see if you can relate to a different type of problem: For a variety of reasons, some people have great difficulty letting themselves think realistically about their condition, much less trying to tackle it. So they may minimize the seriousness of their problem and the impact it has on their life. They may tell themselves that their "habit" is just a nuisance, that no one notices or cares about bald areas or raw skin, or that the problem will just go away by itself at some point, even when there is substantial evidence to the contrary.

Intervention: "I have to face reality about my situation if I am ever going to recover. This doesn't mean condemning myself, just that I have to acknowledge 'the truth, the whole truth, and nothing but the truth' so I can get my life and my self-esteem back."

Excessively Negative Thoughts About Yourself or Others

Misguided thoughts also include those that you may hold about yourself or others. Not surprisingly, such beliefs can have a tremendous negative impact on your moods and self-esteem, which are hurtful secondary effects of BFRBs that can serve as additional stressors and which may lead to even more picking or pulling. Negative beliefs can interfere with your recovery by bringing on depressive feelings and the negative thoughts and behavior patterns that accompany them.

We all have flaws, but when we think that they define us, we sell ourselves way short. Here are some examples: You might see the problem as a sign of a fatal flaw, or of poor character, or as an indication that you lack the requisite willpower to stand up to these temptations and that your problem is the outcome of such inadequacies. One might suppose that this kind of self-criticism would motivate you to stop picking or pulling, but you probably know better. In fact, shame and self-blame are more likely to make the picking or pulling problem worse!

Intervention: "Those beliefs are simply not true! While I may think that it is important to hold myself accountable in life, I'll be more successful if I am kind to myself and learn to hold more rational beliefs than if I berate myself with harsh self-criticism."

Overly negative beliefs about how others may react if they knew about your problem can also get in the way of your recovery. Many people with BFRBs make inaccurate predictions about how others react to sparse hair or damaged skin. Making assumptions about what other people may be thinking is like wearing someone else's prescription glasses. Vision is likely to be blurry and you can misperceive things, *and* you may get hurt in the process.

Likewise, when you make assumptions about others, you can easily misjudge them because, in reality, you cannot be sure of what another person is thinking or feeling about you. Simply guessing and assuming that they notice and focus on the damage, and think badly of you because of it, can contribute to more problems than the actual damage to your skin or hair causes.

And while it is appropriate to take reasonable cosmetic measures such as camouflaging your problem through the use of hairstyles, makeup, and other devices, if you avoid people because you assume that they will reject or judge you, that is a very heavy price to pay. In the end, becoming increasingly isolated from others can be a major contributor to more picking or pulling, and certainly to a less rich life.

Intervention: "I don't know what the future will bring, but if I let fear take over, I will never be happy. I'm going to engage in the world, confide in a few trusted people, and trust that I am not defined by my BFRB!"

Unhelpful Thoughts About Treatment, Healing, and Recovery

We all wish that recovery from BFRBs could be an easy and straightforward process, but unfortunately this is not usually the case. These are complex conditions with deep roots in the nervous system that are not easy to overcome, so it would benefit you to learn about some additional cognitive traps.

You don't know what you don't know. We understand that you have quite a bit of knowledge about your condition; after all, you have been living with it for some time now. However, that doesn't mean that skipping steps is a good idea, especially when it comes to doing self-monitoring. In fact, your belief that you don't need to self-monitor can be an element in the Cognitive domain that undercuts your efforts.

Intervention: We have emphasized that overestimating how much you know about your condition, and underestimating how valuable it will be to gather detailed information about your picking or pulling, can be big mistakes. Since you don't know what you don't know, please try to resist the temptation to skip using *Self-Monitoring Forms* when the time comes to do so. We believe that this crucial step sets the foundation for the entire program, so don't cheat yourself. Avoid disappointment. Gain the highest level of benefit by doing the self-monitoring where we recommend it. Let a thought like this inspire you: "I have more to learn about my BFRB, and new knowledge I gain will help me reach my goal."

Perfectionistic Thinking About Your Recovery

Other types of problematic thoughts and beliefs relate to your recovery and healing process. For instance, you might think that hair or skin should grow back looking perfectly normal, or heal quickly, and that everything should look the way you want it to look. A related belief might be that you will never have the ability to tolerate imperfections, so there is no use in trying. Do these kinds of beliefs feel true to you? They may feel true, but they are likely not true, nor will they serve you well.

Overly critical or perfectionistic thinking can override positive energy, motivation, and hope, so you may be especially vulnerable to feeling discouraged by progress that seems slow, or by slips and setbacks that are likely to occur during your recovery. As best you can, try to be realistic about the task ahead of you. Note perfectionistic thinking when it occurs and use the cognitive interventions that we will describe here and in later chapters to help you fight back and gain the advantage. And while the recovery process will be challenging, trust that you are on the right track. Tolerating the inevitable perceptions of imperfection will help you, not only with regard to your picking or pulling, but in other areas of your life as well. Setting the bar too high is a recipe for disappointment, discouragement, and failure.

Looking ahead, even when you achieve a substantial level of recovery, your ability to live with the imperfections of your skin or hair—and for that matter, the imperfections of life in general—will serve you well. After all, rigid thinking about the way things *should* be is a common human tendency, so cultivating patience and tolerance is something that can benefit us all in many ways. All the while, remember that if you are patient, persistent, and dedicated to the process, you are fully capable of reaching your goal of experiencing life without the added burden of your BFRB.

Intervention: "Feeling imperfect and wanting to do better is natural. My BFRB and my efforts toward recovery are teaching me patience, humility, and compassion for myself and for others."

THE STAGES AND STEPS IN THE PROCESS

As you can see from the discussion above, our mind sometimes tricks us into believing in things that are not true. Just as we can't trust the reality of a mirage, an optical illusion, or a magic trick, sometimes we have to challenge our assumptions and beliefs, especially if we sense they may be steering us in the wrong direction. Cognitive processes and triggers—more than the other BFRB domains—are subtle and elusive, in large part because they are internal, automatic, and compelling. So when it comes to challenging these cognitive triggers, it is especially important for you to focus on them, and make them more accurate and helpful. How will you do this? Read on about Daniel and see how he approaches each step.

Daniel's Story

Daniel, 24 years old, has been bothered by small bumps on his legs and arms since he was in high school. He is self-conscious about them and has avoided wearing shorts, short-sleeved shirts, and bathing suits and going to places like the beach, gym, or pool parties for years. He has been to several dermatologists, and has been told he has a minor skin condition called keratosis pilaris, a harmless but somewhat noticeable condition caused by body oils and impurities that collect in hair follicles. He thinks they are gross and he is afraid that if people see them they will be turned off and might even say something hurtful.

Daniel's dermatologist prescribed a mild medication to aid healing. He only remembers to apply the medicine occasionally. Seeing and feeling the bumps invariably leads him to scratch and pick at them, mostly while getting dressed in the morning or changing into his pajamas at night. On some days he picks and scratches for hours. The result is that he has many scars and open sores on his arms and legs. Daniel is consumed by the idea that he must have smooth skin, and despite evidence to the contrary, he has convinced himself that scratching and picking bumps and scabs will make his skin heal faster and look better.

Stage 1: Building His Awareness

Look below to see how Daniel documented some of the cognitive triggers that set his picking episodes in motion using the

Self-Monitoring Form. So that you can see more easily how your program follows the SCAMP domains, we have included a sensory trigger as well.

Self-Monitoring Form	
Where and What: *Bedroom, getting ready for work.*	
When: *Thurs, April 30*	
Squeezed some gross waxy stuff out of several bumps— glad to get rid of it.	Ⓢ C A M P
I'll never be able to stand the thought of something gross under my skin.	S Ⓒ A M P
If I keep picking and squeezing, I'll make it better.	S Ⓒ A M P
I'll just pick for a minute or two at the big bumps.	S Ⓒ A M P

What I did with the "product": *Used a tissue to wipe off the area and my hands.*

First aware of urge/behavior (0-4): *3*	**Amount that I picked or pulled (0-4):** *3*
0 = Entering situation, 4 = Mid to late in episode	0 = None, 4 = Extreme

Comments: *I never would have guessed that I had so many beliefs that justified my picking and that they were so automatic!*

The above form shows one sensory and three cognitive triggers that Daniel identified and entered on his chart. For the first time, he recognized that certain thoughts and beliefs were contributing to his skin picking, and he was also surprised at how strong and automatic they were. In fact, prior to documenting them he had not really been conscious of them at all.

> **TRY IT!** Ask yourself if any of the unhelpful thoughts or beliefs mentioned above, or other similarly inaccurate or distorted ones, contribute to your pulling or picking. If you want to, you can jot down a few notes, but it is not necessary.

Stage 2: Planning and Preparation

Daniel reviewed the cognitive triggers in his *Self-Monitoring Form*. He noted that in the moment he believed that his picking would help the healing process. At other times he actually gave himself permission to pick by convincing himself that he would only pick for a short time. He recognized that these thoughts were truly inaccurate and unhelpful in pursuing his goal of having healthier skin. He then studied the cognitive interventions in the *Master List of Interventions*. There he saw several ideas that he thought might serve his purpose. He began to consider some possible cognitive interventions—that is, replacements, for inaccurate, distorted, or otherwise unhelpful thoughts and beliefs. Daniel was now convinced that he needed to include some cognitive interventions in his plan. (He called them his "coping statements.")

The way Daniel decided to add these interventions was to put some "coping statements" on his smart phone—rebuttals to the problem thoughts that he had identified. He would read these aloud several times during the day and could eventually recite them from memory. He would recite them at critical times, such as while in his bedroom just prior to changing his clothes.

Here are the coping statements Daniel wrote down in his smart phone:

- I can learn to live with imperfect skin.

- Picking my skin leads to more blood and scabs.

- Skin picking makes my skin less smooth and less healthy.

- Having mild imperfections is better than bloody scabs and more scars.

- Using my skin medication and having patience help my skin become smoother—much more than picking does.

Stage 3: Putting His Plan into Action

Each morning, just prior to taking off his pajamas and getting dressed, and each evening just before he changed into his pajamas (the two times when he most frequently picked at his skin), Daniel read his coping statements from his phone, aloud three times. He recorded the relevant information on his *Action Plan* shown below. Again, in addition to using his cognitive interventions, there is an intervention from the Sensory domain as well. Daniel also noted when he was first aware that he was picking, as well as estimating how much picking he did in his bedroom each day. With this additional information, he could track the relationship between the use of his interventions, the point at which he became aware, and how successful he was each day in controlling his skin picking.

Action Plan							
Situation (Location/Activity): *Bedroom, getting dressed or undressed.*							
When Started: *Monday, Sun., May 4*							
Interventions (Circle Relevant Domain Letters)	S	M	T	W	T	F	S
Problem: *Pick at dry scabs.* Intervention: *Put ointment on scabs.* (S) C A M P	✓	✓		✓	✓		
Problem: *Unhealthy thoughts.* Intervention: *Read coping statements each time I sit on bed.* S (C) A M P	✓		✓		✓		

Awareness (0-4) 0 = Entering setting 4 = Mid to late in episode	1	3	3	4	1	4	4
How much did I pick or pull? (0-4) 0 = None, 4 = Extreme	2	3	3	3	2	4	4
Comments: I am glad that I am now so much more aware of how my beliefs had interfered with my healing. Reading my coping statements is making a difference!							

Perhaps you have noticed that on the days when Daniel did not use any interventions (Friday and Saturday) his awareness scores were "4" and his "skin picking" scores were "3." You might also have noticed that he benefited when he read his coping statements, which he did more than once, and on most days. During this process, he appreciated how much his "thinking as usual" had contributed to the problem that dominated his life. With cognitive interventions (along with interventions from the Sensory domain) now in place, he was beginning to trust that he could gain real power over his skin picking.

> **TRY IT!**   Take a look at the *Master List of Interventions* and circle any of the items that you believe might be of use to you. Feel free to change the wording, or to add other items that apply to you but that are not on the list. Having coping statements on hand in trigger situations will remind you of helpful ways to challenge your cognitive triggers and permission-giving thoughts. You can carry your statements with you on a piece of paper, on index cards, or on your smart phone as Daniel did.

CONCLUSION

We imagine that there have been many times when you have successfully addressed difficult situations by learning to apply new information and engaging in creative problem-solving. Even though skin picking or hair pulling may be a particularly difficult challenge for you, we are confident that you can apply those same abilities and skills as part of your recovery plan.

We hope that reading about the Cognitive domain will help you to become more aware of how inaccurate information and overly negative and distorted thinking has contributed to your problem. We also hope that the list of cognitive alternatives has sparked an "Aha" moment that you will be able to build on. In combination with the other SCAMP domains, what you have learned in this chapter will allow you to build a strong program to gain freedom from your BFRB.

CHAPTER 6

The Affective Domain

Affective experiences—*emotions* and *related internal states*—are so fundamental to being alive that life itself would be virtually unrecognizable without the joys and heartaches, passions and sorrows, excitement and boredom, and elation and despair that we encounter on life's journey. Difficult affective experiences are a part of life, whether or not we have a BFRB condition. We can respond to these affective experiences in a number of healthy ways through the use of appropriate problem-solving and other beneficial approaches. At times, though, we may be tempted to do things that are *not* helpful. Use of alcohol or drugs or eating junk food are a few of the misguided ways in which we might try to manage distress, and for similar purposes some individuals may engage in skin picking or hair pulling. As you have already seen, these efforts to achieve a "quick fix" may provide short-term relief, but they are very likely to have negative long-term consequences.

MANAGING AFFECTIVE TRIGGERS

This chapter explores the Affective domain (the "A" in SCAMP). In it you will learn how your feelings can play important parts in encouraging your BFRB. Particularly important to understand is how short-term relief from unwanted feelings can be provided by picking or pulling, and how these effects reinforce—and thus strengthen—those behaviors. You will also be introduced to a number of healthy alternative activities, ones that can help you through those distressing moments without your having to resort to picking or pulling, or without forcing you to just suffer through the unwanted feelings. Using healthier alternatives for dealing with unwanted emotions can not only help in efforts to overcome your BFRB, they can also help manage the inevitable range of emotional experiences that life presents.

By the end of this chapter we think you will have a pretty good understanding of how experiences within the Affective domain can powerfully influence your BFRB, and how you can learn to manage them without damaging yourself.

DEALING WITH DIFFICULT EMOTIONAL STATES

Uncomfortable emotions can serve us in useful ways by making us aware of problems that need to be addressed and motivating us to do something about them. However, when they become too strong, or last too long, or are unhelpful in other ways, we can become overwhelmed and desperate to find ways to feel better. For many people with BFRBs, picking or pulling can actually be efforts to cope with or to escape from emotional discomfort. For convenience's sake, we have grouped the most common of these emotional triggers into four groups: (1) anxiety and shame; (2) sadness (including hurt feelings), disappointment, and depression; (3) anger, frustration, and irritation; and (4) boredom and restlessness.

Anxiety and Shame

We all feel anxious or worried from time to time about a whole host of things: our health and the health of others, chores, upcoming events, financial obligations, difficulties with our relationships, to name just a few. But your picking or pulling may create an added burden; for in addition to the worries of ordinary, everyday life, you might also endure significant shame—the shame of engaging in problem behaviors that are both visible and self-inflicted.

Perhaps like many others with skin picking or hair pulling problems, you may suffer poor self-esteem due to your BFRB. If so, you may feel so weird or so deeply flawed that you believe you are unworthy of love and respect. Shame and anxiety are intertwined: If you feel excessively anxious or distressed because of your picking or pulling, this can worsen the problem. In addition, worrying about having your damaged skin or hair detected by others and harboring worries about being criticized or rejected create even more problems. In fact, of all the negative emotional consequences associated with BFRBs, shame-fueled anxiety can be the worst.

For example, it is not unusual for people with BFRBs to be so fearful that their problem will be noticed by friends or family members that they may choose to decrease contact with them to keep their secret safe. Prospects for romantic relationships can suffer as well. It is common for individuals who pick or pull to avoid dating because intimate contact could lead to the discovery of their problem—or they may feel they are unworthy of a loving relationship, and so they avoid even entertaining such a possibility. Even those who are in longstanding relationships may take elaborate precautions to prevent or minimize their partner's knowledge of the extent of their problem.

Shame regarding one's picking or pulling can have a negative impact on a person's school or work experience, as well. For students, the time spent on picking or pulling—added to the time it takes to repair or disguise the damage that is done—can make it hard to get to places on time or to complete assignments, not to mention the difficulties of maintaining a healthy social life. Those in the world of work often retreat behind closed doors or spend time in isolation from others to engage in their BFRB, or in efforts to conceal the damage that they have done. Time lost due to these efforts can lead to diminished productivity and to questions in the minds of friends, family members, coworkers, or supervisors. In both school and work settings, many competent and talented individuals try to avoid drawing attention to themselves, and thus opt out of opportunities to give presentations, engage in networking, or take on leadership roles, for fear of being "scrutinized."

Such shame-driven behaviors can increase feelings of loneliness and isolation, which in turn can trigger more BFRB episodes, thus creating even more shame, possibly leading to a downward spiral. To add insult to injury, BFRB-induced shame can prevent many people from pursuing the very help they need.

Interventions that can help with anxiety and shame: Millions of people struggle with BFRBs, yet because of shame and secrecy, many of them—maybe this is true of you, too—have mistakenly believed that they were one of a very few, or even the only one, who had this problem. By gaining greater awareness about the nature of skin picking and hair pulling and how common it is in the human family, you are in a better position to manage the anxiety and shame, to access helpful resources, and to increase the skills that can help you address these problems.

Toward these ends, we recommend that you contact appropriate resources for information and support. Two sources to consider are the TLC Foundation for BFRBs and the Heart and Soul Academy. Information about these and other potentially helpful organizations can be found in the "Resources and References" section at the end of this book.

Sadness, Disappointment, and Depression

Sadness, disappointment, and hurt feelings are inevitable threads in the fabric of human experience. When these emotions are severe or persistent they can deepen into states of hopelessness and depression, familiar problems, unfortunately, among people with BFRBs.

As you may already be aware, lying in bed or staying curled up on the couch are common reactions of depressed individuals, but it isn't hard to see that they are likely to be counterproductive for regaining a healthy state of mind. If taken to an extreme, inactivity of these sorts can develop into lapses in basic self-care, social contacts, and other activities that promote health, happiness, and healing. During vulnerable times, skin picking or hair pulling can offer a degree of comfort and temporary escape from negative feelings, without having to expend a lot of energy. To compound matters, facing the damage caused to one's body often intensifies these negative emotions.

It may seem natural for people to do little more than stay in bed, or stay home and watch TV, to escape significant psychological pain. The problem is that this almost never results in feeling better. For BFRB sufferers, inactivity is likely to provoke further episodes, with even greater damage being a likely outcome.

Interventions that can help with sadness and disappointment: You may already know from your own experience (and research bears this out) that one of the most helpful things people can do when they experience these "down" states is to engage in activities that have an energizing, natural antidepressant effect. Over the years we have been struck by how involvement in certain basic daily activities—including just getting (and staying) out of bed, taking a shower, doing household chores, caring for pets, being outdoors, running errands, helping others, getting together with friends, and engaging in pleasurable activities for pleasure's sake—can lift people's sense of well-being and boost their zest for life.

We realize that those of you who have felt the grip of depression may be thinking, "Don't you think I would do those things if I could?" However, as it turns out, depressed individuals who find ways to engage in productive and pleasurable activities and stay connected with others are more likely to see improvements in their mood than those who think they must wait to feel better before resuming an active life. This is the basis for an effective approach to treating depression called "behavioral activation." So, if you want to improve your mood—make it happen: get up and get out! When you do so, your depression will have a better chance of lifting and your BFRB may very well prove more manageable.

Anger, Frustration, and Irritation

Other stress-related emotions, such as anger and its milder forms, frustration and irritation, can also trigger BFRB episodes in some people. The sources and degrees are varied. Not being able to find our keys, getting caught in a traffic jam when we are already late, having problems at work, or having an argument with a friend are just a few examples.

This isn't to say that these kinds of emotions don't have a purpose in our lives. In fact, at times they can be healthy signals that there is a problem that needs to be addressed, and they can provide a strong motive to address it. They can also help us identify complicated feelings toward others, and recognize situations where we—or those we care about—are being treated unfairly or are in danger.

These feelings are *not* helpful, however, when anger or other negative emotions are unjustified or overly intense, or when they occur too frequently. When you are caught up in these kinds of intense negative emotional states, what do you do with all that energy? If you are like many other people with BFRBs, you might be tempted to lose yourself in skin picking or hair pulling to settle yourself down.

Interventions that can help with anger and frustration: While anger or frustration can be generated by stress, these feelings can also become additional *sources* of stress. During stressful times, your picking or pulling may distract you and help you feel better, at least temporarily. But in the long (or not so long) run you probably realize that this just makes things worse. However, there are ways of handling these situations that will benefit you in the short run *and* in the long run. These can help you achieve a more even composure, so you can face your BFRB and other problems more constructively. For instance, the next time you are upset, instead of resorting to picking or pulling, try doing some *relaxation or breathing exercises* to calm down and keep yourself from getting swept away by those negative emotions (see the *Master List of Interventions* on the website for more details). Or try to identify any feelings and needs that would be helpful to share with others, when communication is in order. Or try to express yourself to others in ways that are appropriate and *assertive*.

Boredom and Restlessness

Boredom and restlessness are part of the human condition. Waiting in line at the store, sitting in traffic, or spending hours working in front of a computer are all situations where boredom and restlessness can—and will—arise. The human body was designed for physical activity, so our nervous system signals us to move when we have been inactive for too long. This means that when we are inactive for a period of time, we can experience restlessness.

This restlessness, which often occurs when we are doing deskwork, having prolonged phone conversations, watching television, or browsing the Internet, can trigger picking or pulling. Why is that? Some writers have suggested that BFRB sufferers are more sensitive to an undesirable degree of stimulation—either too much or too little—than the average person. Some people who feel overly aroused might use hair pulling or skin picking to settle themselves down. Other situations are the opposite: when feeling bored or lethargic, some people engage in their BFRBs seeking higher levels of arousal so they can feel alert, focused, or energized. If any of this sounds familiar to you, your picking or pulling may serve to regulate your level of arousal by providing sensory input that energizes your nervous system, that helps it to relax, or possibly that does both. Although this may temporarily do the job, it takes a substantial toll in repayment.

Interventions that can help boredom and restlessness: You may be tempted to adjust your level of arousal upward by picking or pulling when you feel bored, lethargic, or restless, or conversely, when you feel agitated or distressed, but these needs can be met in healthier ways. Instead of doing something that has harmful effects, try engaging in activities that can either soothe or stimulate your nervous system, depending on your needs at the time, without damaging your body. Some alternative activities offer sensory input via your mouth, hands, or skin—examples would include nibbling on celery, sucking on hard candy, chewing gum, drinking a beverage, or doodling, applying hand lotion, or manipulating an interesting object. You can choose from a number of interventions included in this and other chapters (especially those in the Sensory and Motor domains) when you want to relax or gear up, or in situations where you want your body to be calm but your mind to be alert.

TRANSITION TIMES

Feeling "out of sync" as you shift from one activity to another can also provide affective challenges. This can happen in a variety of circumstances. An example is when you have a number of chores or tasks to do and feel overwhelmed, maybe because you can't decide what to do first. Let's say you have a busy day ahead of you. You need to pick out your clothes and get dressed, eat breakfast, put the dishes in the dishwasher, take a shower, feed and walk the dog, make a doctor's appointment, check the weather, find your keys, take some items to the cleaners, pick up some things at the drug store, wash and iron some clothes, and put gas in the car. But you just don't feel up to facing these demands. The sheer number of chores and how to set your priorities can feel too daunting. So instead of doing any of the above, you might start picking or pulling to give yourself a temporary reprieve from the stress of having to accomplish those tasks.

Another example that might ring a bell is when you are engaging in enjoyable activities, such as watching TV, but know you should be doing something else—some necessary but not particularly desirable activity, such as paying the monthly bills. Too often during this time of internal tension, a BFRB episode provides an easy delay or escape from having to transition from a gratifying to a burdensome activity.

Finally, there may be times when you are undecided about something or stuck in a quandary. For example, "What am I going to do about that neighbor's barking dog that is driving me crazy? Do I just hope it will stop soon? Do I call my neighbor? Do I turn up my music?" You may get stuck at some point and be unable to think of a way to solve the problem. At that moment you may be tempted to seek out some activity that will distract you from the frustration. Your BFRB is always at hand as an alternative. While other people may respond by making a stiff drink or eating a bag of cookies, you may be tempted to escape through picking or pulling.

Interventions that can help those transition times: When you self-monitor, you may discover that you are vulnerable to picking or pulling during transition times of the kinds we have described here. If so, you may benefit from planning ahead. For example, if you pick or pull while reading the paper at home in the morning and thus often end up being late for work, perhaps you could change your routine. You might refrain from reading the paper at the breakfast table and instead take a section of it with you to read on the subway, during a work break, or at lunchtime. If you pick or pull when you are watching TV or browsing the Internet but know that you have housekeeping or work-related tasks to do, perhaps you can do at least some of your chores first and then reward yourself with the enjoyable activity afterwards.

If you get stuck trying to make a decision or solving a problem, go ahead and take a short break—but not a BFRB break! Instead, take a healthy break that involves engaging in some kind of alternative physical activity, such as doing some stretching exercises, going for a brief walk, or just getting up for a beverage. Alternatively, you can temporarily redirect your attention by engaging in an activity that keeps your hands busy, such as filing your nails, working on a crossword puzzle, or rearranging items in your drawers. These kinds of breaks will give your nervous system a chance to "reboot," which may be just what you need to move forward.

The point is to become aware of recurrent situations during which "out-of-sync" affective states predispose you to pulling or picking. Then, by making an effort to alter your routine in ways that are conducive to inner harmony, you are meeting your body's affective needs in healthier ways. In doing so, you will decrease the likelihood of falling into picking or pulling episodes that that you recognize as unhealthy methods of dealing with inner disharmony.

We will now see how Dalia uses the ideas in this chapter to address the factors in the Affective domain that contribute to her hair pulling.

Dalia's Story

Dalia, at age 42, leads a sedentary life. She works in a stressful job and has little time to relax. When she arrives home at night after a long day at work, usually feeling exhausted, she finds something to make for dinner that will be fast and easy to prepare. After dinner she spends time on the computer or watching TV. Still feeling stressed from the day and somewhat bored while lounging, Dalia's hand immediately begins to stroke her hair. One hair is pulled then another and another. Only when she discovers a small pile of hair on the floor, does she retreat upstairs, more upset then before, to get ready for bed. While in the bathroom, she examines the new damage to her scalp hair in the mirror, then sits on the toilet, feeling defeated. As her thoughts settle on the tasks facing her at work the next day, her agitation grows. Feeling upset and overwhelmed, she starts to pull from her pubic hair, and as she does, she has a few minutes of feeling quieter and more distant from her problems.

Once Dalia finally gets into bed, it is later than she had planned and there are not many hours before she has to be up for work. As is true on many nights, she has trouble settling down to fall asleep. She reaches for her head, begins to pull her scalp hair, and this seems to lull her enough to finally drift off to sleep. In the last moments of consciousness, she promises herself that she will try again tomorrow to end her hair pulling.

Stage 1: Building Her Awareness

After learning about the ComB approach, Dalia gained some hope and motivation. First, she spent a few days using the *Self-Monitoring Form*—observing and documenting her patterns of behavior—and then recognized that her evening routine needed to change. Here is what she wrote:

Self-Monitoring Form					
Where and What: Bathroom, evening.					
When: Thursday, 9/15.					
I can't keep my hands from touching and pulling scalp hairs and ones from my pubic area. Once I touch them, I'm doomed	(S)	C	A	M	P
I think that if I don't give in to the urge to pull hairs, I'll never get relaxed.	S	(C)	A	M	P
Pulling my hair is always something to do when I'm alone and bored, or when I'm stressed.	S	C	(A)	M	P
Pulling relieves my stress.	S	C	(A)	M	P
When I'm tired and frustrated because I can't fall asleep, I resort to pulling.	S	C	(A)	M	P
What I did with the "product": Played with the hair and then dropped it on the floor.					

First aware of urge/behavior (0-4): 2	Amount that I picked or pulled (0-4): 4
0 = Entering situation, 4 = Mid to late in episode	0 = None, 4 = Extreme

> **TRY IT!** Consider the information you have learned about features within the Affective domain. Jot down some ideas about how affect may be contributing to your behavior problems.

Stage 2: Planning and Preparation

After reviewing her monitoring form, Dalia identified several factors, especially some in the Affective domain, that served as triggers for her pulling. She also realized that pulling her hair provided her with some desirable *effects* as well. Frustration and stress definitely seemed to initiate some pulling, as did feeling sleepy and tired. The new information was that she was relying on her BFRB to relieve boredom in some circumstances, and to settle herself down in others. *That* seemed important.

She then looked at the *Master List of Interventions* and identified several possibilities that she thought were worth trying. She had always been interested in mindfulness, and now, she thought, might be the time to try out some mindfulness exercises and see if they would help her with frustration and stress in a healthy way. Also, Dalia had wanted to resume knitting, a hobby she used to enjoy. She thought that starting a knitting project might provide her with something to do when she felt bored—she also realized that it would keep her hands busy as well. Finally, Dalia decided to go to bed a bit earlier, after some "settling down" mindfulness exercises to prepare her body for sleep. She kept a book beside her bed and planned to read for fifteen minutes or so if she needed a little more time to settle. Realizing that that seemed a bit risky, she planned to wear light cotton gloves while she read.

> **TRY IT!** Look at the *Master List of Interventions* and circle the "Affective" interventions that you might want to try.

Dalia made a list of ideas she would gather and organize to prepare to put her plan into action:

Buy knitting supplies.

Buy some interesting "fidget toys" and put a box or basket containing the fidget toys near the TV and toilet.

Buy cotton gloves and put them and a book of light reading next to the bed.

Put box or basket near TV, with fidgets and embroidery supplies in it.

Get out a tote bag to put my walking shoes in, and put it by the front door.

Go grocery shopping for food so I can have a quick and healthy meal for dinner.

Find a mindfulness app that I can use regularly.

Write and put my coping card in the container.

Set my phone alarm to ring at 10:30 p.m. to remind me to get to bed by 11:00.

Stage 3: Putting Her Plan into Action

Being armed with her new, ready-to-go plan gave Dalia a new resolve and a determination to implement it. Three times that week she was able to walk, either during her lunch break or once she got home. She discovered that she enjoyed looking for new recipes to try that were tasty and healthier than what she had been eating. Right after dinner, she washed the dishes and brushed her teeth. Only then did she either get on the Internet or watch TV. She found that she enjoyed working on embroidery while watching TV, and using a fidget while on the computer helped her feel less bored. Before getting into bed at 11:00 p.m., Dalia wrote a "To Do" list for the next day so she could get those items off her mind. Here is how her *Action Plan* looked after the first week:

Action Plan							
Situation (Location/Activity): Getting ready for bed, bathroom.							
When Started: Tues, Feb. 3							
Interventions (Circle Relevant Domain Letters)	S	M	T	W	T	F	S
Problem: Free hands. Intervention: Wear gloves. (S) C A M P	✓		✓		✓		✓
Problem: Unhealthy thoughts. Intervention: Read coping cards. S (C) A M P	✓✓		✓✓	✓	✓✓		
Problem: Feeling tired during the day. Intervention: Walk 20 minutes each day. S C (A) M P		✓		✓	✓	✓	✓
Problem: Feeling successful removing hair. Intervention: Knit. S C (A) M P		✓	✓		✓		✓
Problem: Feeling frustrated and stressed. Intervention: Mindfulness for 20 minutes. S C (A) M P		✓	✓		✓		
Awareness (0-4) 0 = Entering setting 4 = Mid to late in episode	2	3	1	3	1	3	1
How much did I pick or pull? (0-4) 0 = None, 4 = Extreme	2	3	2	4	1	4	2
Comments: It wasn't as hard as I thought it might be.							

Dalia did pretty well that week, even though she didn't do as much as she had hoped. She decided to give her plan another week, and then reassess it to see what, if anything, she needed to change. Although the week was not perfect, she found that she was using interventions more than she thought she would and she had more success in limiting her pulling than she had had in years. On Saturday night, she climbed into bed and smiled as she rested her head on her pillow, because she knew that she had started to make some progress. She realized that her progress was modest and that this was not a quick and easy process. She understood that she had to do more, but she finally had hope. That night she slept better than she had in months.

Note: As you read about the plan that Dalia put into action, you may have noticed that there were a number of other possibly useful interventions that she didn't include in her initial plan described above. If so, you are ahead of the game. You have realized that there are always opportunities to add other interventions that might add more power to the program, as well as to discard interventions that just didn't work as well as was hoped.

THE QUESTION OF MEDICATION

Identifying, being aware of, and finding healthy ways to address the kinds of affective factors described in this chapter will help many individuals—perhaps including you—to gain greater control of BFRBs. However, some individuals may need additional help to manage affective elements that contribute to their skin picking or hair pulling. If your emotions are so severe or so volatile that they interfere with your efforts to use the ComB approach successfully, even after repeated efforts to strengthen your program, you may want to consult with an appropriate medical professional—a psychiatrist, nurse practitioner, or family doctor—to see whether medication may help you deal with particularly powerful affective influences on your BFRB. Although medications that reliably address hair pulling or skin picking have yet to be found, some medications do seem to help some individuals regulate their feelings, and thus support their efforts to manage picking or pulling. BFRBs are generally thought to be "neurobehavioral" in nature. This means that there are presumed to be biological, nervous-system factors as well as behavioral ones, with both operating together to generate BFRBs. Therefore, efforts are underway to develop medications that will directly address any underlying biological contributions to these problems.

The neurobiological designation, however, does not fully explain the variations seen in individual expressions of BFRB that have been identified, therefore many experts in the field suspect that there are BFRB "subgroups" that may respond differently to different types of medications. For instance, a significant number of individuals with BFRBs have coexisting (possibly undiagnosed or "subclinical") psychological conditions, such as anxiety disorders or depression, that can be helped by existing medications. These people may benefit from receiving medications that address these related issues and, as a result, find that gaining control of their skin picking or hair pulling is made easier. Otherwise, to restate an unfortunate truth, no prescription medication has been shown in clinical studies to reliably target and effectively reduce BFRBs, though many have been tried.

There is one potential bright spot on the pharmacological front. Recent studies have indicated that N-acetylcysteine (NAC), an over-the-counter food supplement, is a potentially useful medication for hair pulling (the jury is out on its effectiveness for skin picking). While it appears to help many adults with BFRBs (though apparently not children), the good news is that it is safe, has few side-effects, and is relatively inexpensive. Of course, more work needs to be done and some is already underway. With the medical field moving toward "precision medicine"—an approach that fits specific medicines to unique characteristics of each individual—there is hope that, in the case of BFRBs, greater assistance will be provided by medications once they can be chosen in accordance with the relevant characteristics of each individual. How soon the precision-medicine approach will yield benefits for BFRB sufferers is unknown at this time.

We encourage you to keep checking in with the TLC Foundation to read about past, current, and future research on BFRBs and their treatment. As you become more informed, you may want to participate in a study and share what you have learned with your physician. The field is continually moving forward. As in all circumstances, you should first check with your physician before taking any medications. Our hope is that new tools for the effective management and recovery from BFRBs will be found. In the meantime, this book provides you with the best tools that we know of that are available at this time.

CONCLUSION

This chapter has highlighted a number of affective experiences—emotions and related internal states—that can trigger BFRBs and that can have effects that maintain skin picking and hair pulling. It has also offered a number of interventions for you to add to your ComB recovery toolkit. As an added bonus, these interventions can do more than just help you manage your BFRB—they can also enhance your life by improving your mood, your relationships, and your general feeling of well-being. Next, we move to another important domain that is involved when hair pulling and skin picking operate on "automatic pilot"—the Motor domain.

CHAPTER 7

The Motor Domain

The "M" in SCAMP stands for "Motor." The term "motor" refers here to physical movements—in this case, actions that are involved when you pull out hair or pick at your skin. These behaviors, which include touching the target area, searching the scalp or skin for something that is to be removed or altered, and the pick or pull itself, involve complex behaviors and interactions between your nervous system and certain muscles, especially those of your arms, hands, and fingers. Of special interest in this domain is the degree of conscious awareness that accompanies these behaviors, because substantial portions of these behaviors may occur outside of your full awareness.

WHAT ARE MOTOR HABITS?

The Motor domain incorporates a number of factors that involve intentional or automatic movements. Because of the repetitive nature of BFRBs, certain well-practiced behavior patterns become facilitated by the nervous system, leading to the establishment of what we will refer to as "motor habits." As mentioned above, the word "motor" refers to physical movements that occur when your muscles are activated. The word "habit," as we will be using it, is captured by the definition found in the American Heritage Dictionary: a "constant, often unconscious inclination to perform some act, acquired through its frequent repetition."

Thus, motor habits are sequences of movements that do not necessarily require your active awareness in order to be performed. Sometimes they can be triggered by external events, as when we unknowingly tap our foot while listening to music. Other times, internal thoughts or feelings can trigger a motor habit, such as gritting our teeth while remembering an incident that makes us furious. As the term applies to hair pulling and skin picking, motor habits can refer to physical movements that occur outside of your full awareness (that is, "unconscious" movements or movements we're only partially aware of) or behaviors and sequences of behavior that you are aware of but may find difficult to resist due to your repeated practice of these actions over time. In either case, motor habits can be major contributors to the maintenance of your pulling and picking.

Neuropathways and Motor Habits

Motor activities (sequences of physical movements) occur when certain areas of the brain communicate with other areas of the brain to initiate movements in specific muscle groups. If these same behavior sequences occur repeatedly, a chemical and electrical pathway can become established, allowing the message to travel more easily and quickly from one area of our brain to another, through other parts of the nervous system, and then to our muscles. To illustrate this process, we can think of a forest as a metaphor for the nervous system's network of neurons. Without any paths, moving through a dense forest is slow going. However, once a trailblazer creates a path, it is much easier to use it. Eventually, walking through the forest on this trail requires very little effort; one can simply follow the trail without having to think much about it. This is similar to what happens in your nervous system. When a neuromuscular pathway has become well established, the neurons are able to communicate quickly and easily from one area of the brain to the next, and to the muscles that execute the behavior sequence. As you know from a previous chapter, the sensory system gets involved as well, sending feedback to the brain, and thereby completing the cycle. This makes it very easy for a person to repeat certain behavioral patterns—both desirable and undesirable—without the requirement of conscious control or even any degree of awareness.

In addition to establishing facilitated nervous system pathways (neuropathways), when behaviors are repeated numerous times, the muscles that are used become trained and strengthened. These behavior patterns can be performed routinely and without conscious monitoring because our nervous system pathways and muscles are working together, thereby creating a "motor habit." This is why, when we are in our familiar surroundings, our motor habits allow us to do one activity while being completely engrossed in thinking about something entirely different. You may have had the experience, for example, of being so deep in thought that you may not even remember brushing your teeth or driving past familiar sites on your way to work. These habits can also include other complex activities, such as playing a musical instrument, typing, dancing, or playing tennis. In these cases, the skills may be hard to learn at first, but they become easier and more fluid over time and require less conscious monitoring or effort due to repetition. Because they are so well practiced, they can be quite resistant to change, which anyone who has tried to break a bad habit can tell you. This is one major reason why you will need to plan well and work hard to overcome the stubborn persistence of your well-established BFRB, a pattern of behavior that you may have practiced for untold hours, and now so desperately want to eliminate.

ARE BFRBS JUST "BAD HABITS"?

In common practice, the word "habit" can also refer to predictable routines. Some habits, like saying "Thank you" at appropriate times, can be thought of as "good habits." Minor examples of "bad habits" include bothersome behaviors such as leaving the top off of the toothpaste or dropping dirty clothes on the floor. But the term has also been used for behaviors associated with more serious problems, such as smoking, overeating, hoarding, and gambling. Because the general public has become more educated about such problems, many people now understand that these problems are more than "bad habits," and that they may be virtually impossible to resist by the use of willpower alone.

Unfortunately, this same level of appreciation for the persistence of problem behaviors does not always apply to BFRBs. This is largely because the general population is not yet as knowledgeable about hair pulling or skin picking as they are with overeating, gambling, and shopping compulsions. Some people assume that people suffering from BFRBs simply have a bad habit that is within their power to control, and that if they are unable to do so, it is a sign of weakness of character. Other people believe that even if pulling and picking disorders are more complex and difficult to manage than they may seem at first glance, they still maintain that individuals who pick or pull should be capable of overcoming these problems through sheer willpower. Where does the truth lie?

THE HABITUAL ROUTINES AND CHAINS OF EVENTS IN HPD AND SPD

We still do not fully understand all of the conditions that *cause* picking or pulling problems in any given individual. Generally, though, experts consider these conditions as neurobehavioral disorders with origins not yet understood, but that are assumed to involve an inborn vulnerability, expressed in response to life experiences that have not yet been identified. So, even though much remains to be learned about the causes of HPD and SPD, at least we do know quite a bit about a variety of factors that contribute to their *maintenance*. In this chapter, we will underscore how powerful motor habits facilitate and maintain the scratching, pulling, and picking at target areas. Remember that BFRBs are not just simple problems or "bad habits" that are easily overcome. Nor is it reasonable to expect that you, or anyone else with a picking or pulling problem, will be able to overcome it by willpower alone. However, by understanding the nature of the Motor domain, you will gain vital information about additional mechanisms that make your problem seem unstoppable.

We can start by pointing out three important aspects of the Motor domain that will help you understand why this domain is so important and why it must be addressed.

First, BFRB episodes usually involve a predictable and ingrained chain of events that play out in a predictable way. What follows is one possible chain of events, much of which can occur without conscious awareness:

1. You enter a trigger situation, one that is somehow linked with pulling or picking in your experiences.

2. A cue, perhaps visual or tactile, or an internal experience people usually describe as an "urge," sets the BFRB chain of behaviors in motion.

3. With fingertips or by sight you search for a hair or area of skin that will be your "target."

4. You locate the "target" and proceed with picking or pulling ("extraction").

5. You manipulate, bite, swallow, examine, toss, or otherwise dispose of the hair or bit of skin you secured. You may enjoy the immediate effect these activities have on your emotions, or maybe good feelings have eluded you—in either case, repeated pulling or picking continues.

6. Eventually the episode ends because one or more of a variety of external or internal factors has ended the sequence (for example, someone interrupts you, or you become aware of the damage you have done).

Second, the more you can avoid, delay, or thwart the *first or earliest* link in the chain of behaviors, the more successful your efforts will be. To use an analogy, you can think of the ingrained pattern of each BFRB episode as a kind of "rut in the road." If you know the rut is there, you can avoid it by driving around it or taking a different path. If you are not able to do so, once you slide into the rut, it is almost impossible to get out of it until your vehicle reaches the end of the rut. Likewise, it is harder to stop the BFRB chain the deeper you go into the sequence of linked behaviors. Early intervention is a key to success, and this is why we strongly encourage you to use your interventions in a preemptive or preventative manner *as soon as you enter any trigger situation.* In this way, movement beyond the first or early links in the chain can be halted. Don't fall for the idea that you don't have to use interventions because you believe that you can do fine without them. That, unfortunately, is a recipe for disappointment.

Third, interventions that are described here, operating within the Motor domain, will help you in a number of ways: (1) They create a barrier that thwarts unconscious performance of BFRB activities, thereby helping to activate awareness. (2) They make it difficult, or less appealing, to pull or pick. (3) They keep your hands busy in beneficial ways. We will explore these features in greater detail later in this chapter.

THE CONTINUUM OF AUTOMATIC AND FOCUSED PULLING AND PICKING

As we have said, for many people, elements within their BFRB chain of behaviors occur outside of awareness a significant portion of the time. For these individuals, SPD or HPD may seem to follow uncontrollable patterns of runaway behavior—ones that seem to operate on automatic pilot much of the time. Other individuals may be very much aware of the process of picking or pulling much or almost all of the time, but they still may be unable to gain control because of the "driven" quality of their behavior, or because they have felt unable to resist the temptation of achieving the desirable effects they derive from them.

For the purpose of illustration, we will separate automatic and focused styles in our examples. Sometimes the BFRB experience is largely unconscious, occurring with attention focused on some other activity. Hands seem to have a "mind of their own," and don't require conscious control. This is the automatic style. In other cases, the BFRB is performed with full consciousness and intent, with some people reporting that they go into a "trancelike state" with a hyperfocus on the activity itself. But in reality, most pullers and pickers experience a combination of the two styles. Some may experience episodes of both sorts, or they may have single episodes that blend both styles. Both of these varieties are described as "combination style."

Mainly Automatic Pulling and Picking

When your pulling or picking occurs outside of conscious awareness, the behaviors are referred to as *automatic*. This typically occurs when you are engaged in a sedentary, routine activity such as reading, watching TV, using the computer, or contemplating the solution to a problem. Without even thinking about it, your hands can drift to the target site. The behavior can start automatically, and link by link, a chain reaction takes place, with greater awareness occurring as the sequence plays out. Because of these features, increasing your degree of awareness as early as possible in the chain is a key element in the recovery process. Awareness is thus a crucial component of your program, because it will enable you to uncover and control elements of your BFRB that typically fly under the radar. Doesn't it makes sense that it will be harder to gain control of any aspect of your behavior if you are not aware of when you are doing it?

Interventions to increase your awareness: To emphasize an important point, increasing your awareness is important for overcoming BFRBs, even if you are engaging mainly in focused pulling or picking, because automatic behaviors early in the sequence often set an episode in motion. And increasing awareness is especially vital if you tend to have significant bouts of automatic BFRB activity.

As you have seen previously, a useful first step in increasing awareness involves monitoring the details and sequences of your BFRB episodes. By raising your awareness in this way, you can get better at anticipating, and thereby be better prepared to limit, the automatic aspects of the motor habit. This is an important step in developing an effective recovery plan.

Mainly Focused Pulling and Picking

Now we will consider individuals for whom highly focused performance of the BFRB represents the lion's share of their problem. Focused pulling or picking tends to be driven by one or more of the following factors: the desire for pleasurable or interesting sensations; the attempt to reduce or eliminate unwanted emotions or other unpleasant internal experiences; or the effort to achieve some desired goal, such as perfect hairline symmetry or the correction of an unwanted feature of hair or skin. These are common motives for people who are very conscious that a BFRB episode is underway. However, please note that *even for people who are aware of most of what drives their picking or pulling, there are likely to be at least some automatic elements, such as hands moving to hair or skin, with fingertips searching for likely targets, without that person's awareness.*

When awareness is present: If your pulling or picking is almost entirely of the focused style, can you always anticipate when the episodes will occur ahead of time? For most people the answer is "no." Even individuals with a primarily focused style gain an increased ability to control their BFRB as their awareness increases. Contributors to BFRBs that often go undetected within the Motor domain include physical postures that position fingers near hair or skin, fingers exploring hair or skin, or even picking or pulling that had begun before the person realized it. Take, for example, a case of an individual with an eyebrow-pulling problem. The individual may be reading and absent-mindedly running her fingertips across her eyebrow. Her fingers may detect a bothersome short, sharp hair.

Unknowingly, her fingers may already be attempting to grab the short, bothersome hair without success. Now, suddenly, she snaps to full alertness, gets up, goes to the bathroom, picks up her tweezers, and looks in the mirror to pull out that annoying hair, which she does. But then she moves on to pull out any others she can find that feel sharp or prickly.

Automatic elements of focused pulling episodes: As noted above, even when there is focused picking or pulling, automatic touching is often an early link of the chain. This can be especially problematic in situations where posture or body position allows hands easy access to the hair or skin. An example of this would be a student who can't stop picking at callouses on his feet, yet he usually reads on his couch with his book resting on his curled legs and his bare feet inches from his free hand.

In your case, once potential targets are identified either visually or by touch, the ingrained and persistent motor habits created over days, months, or years of repetition, set the stage for the next link in your behavioral chain. And once the familiar sequence is underway, you may feel helpless to stop, even if you are fully aware of what are you doing. Because there are likely to be at least some automatic elements involved in highly focused behavior, it is important that you increase your awareness of the subtle motor habits that set the BFRB chain of behaviors into motion. Various wrist-watch-like feedback devices are now on the market. While not true barriers, they can alert the user of movements associated with BFRB performance and may have additional benefits for record-keeping.

INTERVENTIONS THAT CAN HELP YOU ADDRESS MOTOR TRIGGERS

There are a number of interventions available to help you to increase your awareness and thereby discourage automatic aspects of your picking or pulling. Some of these interventions create barriers that impede easy access and provide sensory feedback to help you heighten your awareness. This can be accomplished by employing interventions that make picking or pulling more difficult to accomplish, less rewarding, or by keeping your hands busy in some other activity. Some ideas are contained in the brief descriptions that follow. Others can be found in the *Short List of Interventions* in the Appendix of this book and in the much longer *Master List of Interventions* on the New Harbinger website.

Create Barriers to Protect Your Hair and Skin

Easy access of your hands to the target areas of your body is one element that helps maintain BFRBs over time. As you develop your recovery program, plan to use a variety of interventions to increase your awareness of early links in the BFRB chains. These can have another benefit as well: They can "buy time" for you to think of additional ways to stop the picking or pulling episode from moving forward. Barriers can be as simple as adhesive bandages placed on the fingertips or used to cover wounds that are easy targets for repeated picking. Clothing items such as hats, gloves, socks, long-sleeved shirts, or tights can serve similar purposes.

Think about barriers that might suit your situation. Let's say that that you frequently pick at skin irregularities on your arms while relaxing and reading at home in the evening. Perhaps, through previous self-monitoring, you noted how often that your fingers moved to scabs and dry patches of skin on your arms. For this example, you also identified the specific triggers for picking, including relaxing and pleasure reading after supper. In this case, by focusing on the Motor domain you might choose to place bandages on your thumb and first two fingers before entering that situation where you are vulnerable. Then, when your fingers travel to your arms, the bandages will trigger awareness. Of course, nothing will stop you from removing them if you choose to, but you *have* interrupted unconscious links in the chain, and that will give you the chance to put potentially useful interventions from other domains into play.

Make It Difficult or Less Appealing to Grasp, Pull, or Pick

You have probably noticed that once BFRB episodes are underway it can become extremely difficult to stop them in their tracks. The search for pleasurable sensations or other desirable outcomes— for example, removing unwanted hairs, getting pus out of a pimple, or deriving some satisfying sensations from the extracted bits of skin or hair—typically leads to further links in the BFRB chain of behaviors. By altering the picking or pulling site, thereby making it less appealing to touch, grasp, or pull hair, or to make picking or even touching the skin less appealing, you can further increase awareness and guard against automatic behaviors.

For example, if working at the computer is a particular problem for a person with a hair-pulling problem, it would be wise for her to plan ahead. Prior to sitting down at the computer, she might take a quick shower and wash her hair. When she gets out of the shower, she could apply a conditioner and leave it on her hair, making it slippery and probably less appealing to pull. She could also wrap her head in a towel, adding another barrier to automatic behaviors. While she has the conditioner on her hair and with her head well wrapped, she can look forward to some pull-free work time. With multiple barriers in place, she has altered the likelihood of pulling in a number of ways—all to her advantage. As a bonus, she has helped make her hair healthier in the process.

Keep Your Hands Busy in Beneficial Ways

Many people find that even when they are attempting to increase awareness, movements toward the picking or pulling site may happen very quickly and without warning. By now you are aware of certain environments where you routinely engage in pulling or picking. Just entering into one of those environments can trigger the early links in the sequence of behaviors, with or without your awareness. Those BFRB neuropathways and motor memories are always ready to fly into action!

You can retrain your brain and muscles by engaging in other motor activities, competing ones, that keep your hands busy or away from potential target sites. If those alternative activities are interesting, pleasurable, or otherwise gratifying, as well as incompatible with picking and pulling, you will find that they can do more than just keep your hands busy. They can also provide beneficial stimulation and sensations to your hands and fingers. Be especially attentive to activities that you anticipate will provide you with pleasurable visual or tactile experiences, as these will add benefits from the Sensory domain.

Let's say, for instance, that watching TV when alone usually leads to pulling or picking before you are even aware of it. In these situations, you might consider keeping your hands otherwise occupied by engaging in a non-self-damaging alternative activity. You can draw, doodle, take notes, or manipulate an interesting item from the expanded lists we have provided. Keeping your hands busy in these ways will interfere with the automatic performance of old motor habits and will help develop new ones that replace problem behaviors. This approach will be especially helpful if you use these methods as preventative measures early in the BFRB sequence. Manipulating items in these and many similar situations can help protect you, especially when you are engaged in sedentary activities that leave you—and your hands—feeling restless.

PUTTING AN INITIAL PLAN INTO PLACE

Here is how Aisha developed better awareness and created an initial plan that focused on the Motor domain to help her manage her skin picking.

Aisha's Story

Aisha, 37, is waiting in line at the bank and has a number of questions regarding her account. As she thinks about her questions and waits her turn, her hand travels up her arm. Her fingers reach under her short sleeve and she begins to pick absent-mindedly at a scab on her upper arm. Deep in thought, her fingers move and locate a second bumpy patch and pick at that spot, as well. While her mind is on banking business, her hands travel further, searching for irregularities. After almost fifteen minutes she has still not yet reached the bank teller, but she is shocked into awareness when she sees blood appearing through the pink sleeves of her blouse. Feeling ashamed, she looks around to see if anyone notices the bleeding. She quickly exits the line and leaves the bank without completing her business there.

Stage 1: Building Her Awareness

Here is Aisha's *Self-Monitoring Form*, which will illustrate how documenting certain details of each BFRB episode increased her awareness, which in turn increased her ability to develop an effective self-help plan.

Self-Monitoring Form	
Where and What: At the bank, waiting in line.	
When: Wednesday, 7/8	
My arms were itching.	(S) C A M P
It was warm. I wanted to wear a short-sleeved blouse and thought I'd be able to resist picking.	S (C) A M P
Feeling stressed and annoyed while waiting in a long line at the bank.	S C (A) M P
My arms were folded, so my hands were close to my upper arms.	S C A (M) P
I realized that my hands were empty, so they were free to scratch and pick my arms.	S C A (M) P

What I did with the "product": *Nothing*	
First aware of urge/behavior (0-4): *3* 0 = Entering situation, 4 = Mid to late in episode	**Amount that I picked or pulled (0-4):** *3* 0 = None, 4 = Extreme
Comments: *I hadn't realized how many times my hands were folded, which set the stage for picking.*	

By documenting several of her picking episodes, Aisha realized that there were a number of other situations in which a similar chain of behaviors occurred. These included the waiting room of the dentist's office, in a taxi, at the checkout line in the supermarket, and so on, during which her picking episodes started with her hands unconsciously traveling to areas of her upper arms, shoulders, and back—an early link in her BFRB chain. She also began to notice other kinds of triggers that set her picking events into motion.

> **TRY IT!**   Think about automatic and focused aspects of your picking and pulling, including when you usually become aware that you are picking or pulling. Jot down any useful information that you discover about your own chains of behavior.

Stage 2: Planning and Preparation

By gaining insight into aspects of her picking of which she had been largely unaware, Aisha took a big step toward gaining further control over her problem. Now she began thinking about ways to address the automatic elements of her SPD. The next step would be for her to identify useful interventions that she could use to break the BFRB chain before it really got started—and to use them as early in the sequence as possible, or ideally to prevent it from starting in the first place. She had some ideas for interventions that she came up with on her own, and got some more from the *Master List of Interventions* on the New Harbinger website.

Aisha then focused on the elements she identified that led to the picking incident at the bank. These were:

- Itchy arms. (S)CAMP

- Believing she was safe from picking while wearing a short-sleeved shirt. S(C)AMP

- Feeling stressed and annoyed. SC(A)MP

- Resting with arms folded, with hands touching her upper arms. SCA(M)P

- Hands empty and free to scratch arms. SCAM(P)

Aisha was now more aware of the details of her skin-picking episode, including the involvement of other domains, so she decided to include them in the interventions she would try. The interventions were:

- Apply anti-itch cream morning and evening. (S)CAMP

- Note on closet door: "You are vulnerable wearing short-sleeved blouses—choose long or elbow-length ones." S(C)AMP

- Do deep, slow breathing when feeling stressed. SC(A)MP

- When alone at home, wear an elbow brace to remind me to keep my hands away from my upper arms. SCA(M)P

- Play a game on my phone or do a crossword puzzle to help keep my hands busy while I wait. SCAM(P)

Aisha was beginning to have hope. She knew that there was still a lot ahead of her, but thinking about how these interventions might help gave her a more positive outlook. Next, she had to make some preparations, so she made a list and did the following things the very next day:

Buy anti-itch cream.

Put note on closet door.

Look up and print out some breathing exercises and practice them.

Buy an elbow brace.

Download an interesting game to my phone

Put a crossword puzzle and pen in my purse.

TRY IT!   Look at the *Master List of Interventions* and mark some interventions you might like to try for times that your hands "have a mind of their own."

Stage 3: Putting Her Plan into Action

Aisha was starting to get excited about trying out her plan, so first she recorded her plan using an *Action Plan* form. The following day she put her plan into motion. She used it for a full week, assessed how it went, and made a few modifications. Here is what her form looked like, along with her comments:

Action Plan							
Situation (Location/Activity): *Waiting.*							
When Started: *Sun., June 12*							
Interventions (Circle Relevant Domain Letters)	S	M	T	W	T	F	S
Problem: *Itchy skin.* Intervention: *Anti-itch cream.* (S) C A M P	✓		✓		✓		✓

Problem: Feeling impatient. Intervention: Deep breathing. S C (A) M P		✓		✓	✓	✓	✓
Problem: Bare arms. Intervention: Wear long sleeves. S C A (M) P	✓	✓	✓	✓	✓		
Problem: Arms folded. Intervention: Wear elbow brace. S C A (M) P	✓		✓	✓	✓		
Problem: Empty hands. Intervention: Do crossword puzzle or play game on phone. S C A (M) P		✓					✓
Awareness (0-4) 0 = Entering setting 4 = Mid to late in episode	2	3	2	2	1	3	3
How much did I pick or pull? (0-4) 0 = None, 4 = Extreme	2	3	2	2	1	4	2

Comments: I put the lotion on quickly and then immediately got dressed (or put on long-sleeved pj's). I did a crossword puzzle on my phone while waiting for different things, and it helped. (I also looked at my emails—that helped as well, so I will add it to my list next to the crossword puzzle. All in all, it was good—my worst day was on Fri. when I only used two interventions and wore short sleeves (big mistake), and didn't wear the elbow brace while I watched TV!

ADDING "M" TO YOUR SCAMP TOOLKIT

In previous chapters, you learned about a variety of possible tools that fall within three critical domains: Sensory, Cognitive, and

Affective. Presumably, you have already considered some of them for inclusion in your SCAMP toolkit.

In this chapter, we have described the role of motor habits in BFRB disorders. You have learned how these habits can bypass your conscious awareness and play an important part in your picking or pulling. Furthermore, you now understand how even highly focused pulling has at least some automatic elements that should be identified and addressed. You have also learned some specific techniques designed to help you retrain your brain and muscles by impeding and redirecting your movements, using barriers, and keeping your hands busy with activities that are incompatible with pulling and picking.

The Motor domain techniques interrupt the BFRB sequence and give you time to use additional interventions from other domains. We hope that you will give serious consideration to including them in your *Action Plan*, as these will likely prove to be critical ingredients for achieving the success you desire.

In the next chapter you will learn about the final domain in SCAMP—"P" for "Place." Upon completion of the next chapter, you will possess the full complement of the tools within each of the SCAMP domains and know how to use them. At that point you will be ready to design your master plan, put it in play, and be well prepared to overcome your BFRB!

CHAPTER 8

The Place Domain

In this chapter we will complete the SCAMP domains, by focusing on the "P," which refers to "Place." But as you will soon see, "place" includes many aspects of your external environment that have an impact on behavior—not just the physical location. In the first half of this chapter you will learn about features in your physical environment that encourage picking and pulling. The second half of the chapter will introduce you to interventions designed to meet the challenges of environmental features that are relevant to your picking or pulling.

ENVIRONMENTAL HAZARDS

A variety of environmental factors, usually in combination with ones from other domains, can create high-risk situations for people with HPD or SPD. Most obviously, these factors include places that have become associated with hair pulling or skin picking. However, they also include factors such as isolation from others, particular times of day, involvement in sedentary activities, performance of daily activities associated with pulling or picking, and the availability of certain implements that can trigger or encourage BFRB activity. As you read about each of these factors, think about which ones apply to you.

Privacy

If you are like the vast majority of people, you find it very uncomfortable to be observed engaging in hair pulling or skin picking. You may worry about being seen, being judged, or being confronted by someone about these activities. It is likely that you require a measure of privacy to feel comfortable engaging in your BFRB. Some individuals isolate themselves for significant amounts of time, because they, like many others, require a measure of concentration in a private place where there are few distractions—especially when they are in a *focused* mode.

The desire to be alone when engaging in picking or pulling leads people to seek out places that provide the necessary degree of isolation. A private office, bathroom, bedroom, or some other place that is out of the way, or that has a door to close, can provide the privacy necessary to indulge freely in a BFRB. Total separation from others isn't always necessary. A car, for instance, can provide the sense of concealment and anonymity in what feels like a personal space. Those who have small children may act as if their behavior is invisible to their children, and that their picking or pulling in various areas within their house will go undetected even when they are within their children's observation range.

Most of us have reasonable, healthy needs for seclusion or privacy under certain circumstances. For example, personal hygiene activities are likely to be done most comfortably when we are not observed by others. Even less sensitive tasks, such as work on an important project that may require full focus and concentration, would lead most people to isolate themselves from distractions in order to maximize the quality and efficiency of their work. Of course, when in our bathroom, we all prefer the degree of privacy that the confines of the private space provide. You also may realize that you are very vulnerable because of the very nature of the isolating spaces—the closed door, the private place, the sense of being completely alone, and so on—that can set the stage for an episode of skin picking or hair pulling to occur.

Certain Times of Day

Time of day may also be an external, contributing factor for many who pull their hair or pick their skin. For example, some people find that they are more likely to engage in these behaviors in the early morning, before the activities and demands of the day begin. They can "get stuck" in hair pulling or skin picking while grooming, dressing, or otherwise preparing for the day and thereby lose precious time in otherwise busy schedules.

Other individuals find that returning home after a day at work or school can be challenging. At such times, it may be hard to leave thoughts and feelings about their day and their work or other experiences behind. It may be difficult to shift gears or otherwise disengage from the day's effects and prepare to face tasks that require attention at home, such as sorting mail, paying bills, preparing dinner, and other routine tasks and family obligations. For many, skin picking or hair pulling can serve as a break from the hustle-bustle and tensions of the day.

Another time that you may find challenging is bedtime. Ending a day, however demanding it may have been, usually means feeling tired, trying to wind down, and preparing for sleep. Though seemingly simple and natural, these factors lead many individuals to be quite vulnerable to picking and pulling in the nighttime. Routine evening activities, such as washing hands and face in front of the bathroom mirror, getting undressed, putting on sleep attire, and lying awake in bed, may provide moments of vulnerability and temptation. The sight of exposed skin, scabs, blemishes, or bumps, or hairs that seem ripe for pulling can easily break down resistance and provoke damaging episodes.

Sedentary Activities and Daily Routines

Many people find that certain confining or sedentary activities are conducive to engaging in picking or pulling. Sitting in the family room and watching TV, reading in the living room, surfing the Internet, or talking on the phone may be powerful trigger situations.

While we are sitting quietly in a comfortable position, idle hands may be prone to become restless and search for hairs to play with or for a small, rough patch of skin to scratch off and smooth out. For some, such episodes can be fleeting. For others, they might lead to hours-long BFRB episodes.

We all know what it is like to have habits and routines. These involve sets of behaviors that occur semiautomatically in familiar settings. How and why this is so requires a quick and simplified view of the biology behind the scenes. As noted earlier, as soon as we enter a familiar environment, certain established brain pathways are engaged. These guide the performance of well-practiced sequences of behaviors. Once activated, such routines require little conscious effort for the sequences of behaviors to unfold. A simple example is how our hands know pretty much what they are to do while we rinse them after mundane tasks. Another example is the common morning routine of brushing our teeth. When we go into the bathroom to brush our teeth, we reach for the toothbrush and the toothpaste while thinking about other things—or even while still half asleep—yet we have few problems completing the task. Because of the well-practiced nature of the behavior, a person with a history of engaging in skin picking in such situations, however, might habitually glance in the mirror to check for facial imperfections. The detection of such potential targets can lead to the obvious next step—take action. As one thing leads to another, this can easily develop into a BFRB episode that is virtually out of control. With enough repetition of this behavioral sequence, just entering the bathroom can set off a chain of semiautomatic behaviors: looking in the mirror, detecting skin flaws, picking at the flaws, searching for other flaws, and so on. This pattern can become part of the morning tooth-brushing routine. The chain of behaviors has become coded into the neuropathways that facilitate future episodes of this routine. In this way, the environment itself "cues" or silently directs the person to initiate the behavior chain that has become a facilitated and therefore ingrained part of that person's morning routine.

Implements

Implements or other environmental features that can facilitate skin picking or hair pulling are often found in particular places. These include bright lights, mirrors (particularly magnifying mirrors), tweezers, needles, and pins.

The bathroom often includes a considerable number of these features, and is thus a real danger zone for many vulnerable individuals. Looking into a mirror with bright lights shows all manner of small imperfections—errant hairs or small irregularities of the skin, such as bumps, blemishes, large pores, blackheads, whiteheads, and skin discoloration, just to name a few.

The availability of tweezers also may pose a serious challenge for many people. After identifying imperfections, tweezers facilitate the removal of specific hairs or can be used to pick deeply at blemishes. Once either is started, they can be difficult to stop. Some of our patients are so reliant on their tweezers, magnifying mirrors, pins, and needles that we have come to call those items "implements of destruction," because that is what they have become for them. Though they may have intended to remove just a few errant hairs or to pick at just one skin irregularity, many find themselves unable to stop, and wind up with far more damage to skin or hair than they had expected.

People who pick at their skin using tweezers, needles, or pins to dig deeply usually have the goal of "getting something out" of blemishes such as blackheads or pus. They might use needles to dig under the skin in a misguided effort to promote the healing process in an area where pimples, swelling, and other signs of damage are already present. This practice, far from encouraging quicker healing, typically leads to bleeding, sores, scabs, infections, swelling, and even scarring. Blemishes heal better and faster when they are left to the natural healing process. Squeezing and picking is ultimately counterproductive, often leading to deepening infection and heartbreaking degrees of damage to the skin.

INTERVENTIONS FOR MANAGING PLACE

No wonder many people get discouraged when many daily environments are so "BFRB friendly"! Because many situations involve the familiar ingredients of privacy, repetitive practice, hands free and available, adequate time, and access to implements, all represent crucial challenges to efforts meant to overcome HPD and SPD. These locations and situations will become the battlegrounds in your campaign to regain healthy hair and skin. Fortunately, there are many opportunities to address these contributors to your problem in practical ways. These will add to your chance for success in your self-help effort. Here is where you start.

Increase Your Awareness

Increasing your awareness is just as important with the Place domain as it is with the others. Becoming aware of the triggers that help launch picking or pulling in varieties of environments is an important first step. Take note of locations and activities where your hands are idle and become familiar with the chains of behaviors as they occur in situations where pulling hair or picking skin is highly likely to occur as part of your daily routines.

Be as diligent as a newspaper reporter or a scientist would be, in gathering new information or insights that come your way when observing your behavior. You may discover, as you focus on the connections between environmental variables and your behaviors, that these factors play a much bigger role than you might have suspected.

Make Changes Within the Environment

As you become more aware of the places that are challenging for you, you will want to consider how you can organize your physical spaces differently. Even small physical changes can have a big impact for many people. By using increased awareness to make these kinds of adjustments, you can reduce your vulnerable "private time," keep your hands busy and your body more active, and thereby disrupt the automatic nature of your routine.

Make the environment less private: Changing the usual place where you sit from a pulling-prone or picking-prone place to a less "BFRB-friendly" place is an excellent way to make some initial changes. A number of our college students have found it helpful to change their studying locations from their dorm room to the dorm lounge, and from a private library study carrel to the main reading room. Another way to decrease isolation would be to leave doors ajar that ordinarily might be closed. This may not be practical for activities that require privacy, such as dressing, toileting, and bathing, but it may be still be a change worth considering at other times, such as when you are brushing your teeth, washing up, or putting on makeup, as well as when you are studying. If this idea does not appeal to you, however, one alternative might be to limit the amount of time you spend behind closed doors, perhaps even setting a timer to go off after an interval that is appropriate for the activity.

Change your location: Sedentary activities, ones that are performed while sitting for extended periods, are highly conducive to engaging in BFRBs. So altering long intervals of sitting by including more physical activity can help make the skin and hair less available to restless hands. Taking frequent breaks that include stretching, walking around, or going up stairs can divert nervous energy that might otherwise serve as fuel for the BFRB. Be aware that these suggestions have advantages in other domains as well as in the Place domain. Consider taking a walk down the hall, doing occasional stretching exercises, or taking short "yoga breaks" while studying, to keep your body and nervous system tuned and healthy. If these suggestions seem too ambitious, consider smaller changes within your environment, like putting nail-grooming supplies, needlepoint or knitting materials, or some "fiddle toys" within arm's reach of where you usually sit to watch TV. If it fits your situation, you may try using a different bathroom from the one ordinarily used for toileting and bathing (*and* picking or pulling) when you put on your makeup, brush your teeth, or wash your face. If this is impractical, then try changing the order in which you usually perform daily tasks. Even small changes to your routine can pay big dividends. Note that many of the suggestions provided here draw from a number of the SCAMP domains. This works to your advantage and we hope that this encourages you to use varieties of interventions, covering a number of domains, to help you prevail in situations where your BFRB now rules.

Rid yourself of implements: Some elements within the environment have inherent dangers for those with BFRB issues. As we have seen, the privacy afforded by one's bathroom can set the stage for prolonged and intense scrutiny of hair and skin. Add the presence of certain grooming implements, such as tweezers, bright lights, and mirrors—especially magnifying mirrors—and you have a perfect storm of factors that can make a trip to the bathroom turn into a devastating experience.

Reducing the light intensity in your bathroom, by removing some light bulbs or finding a dimmer alternative to fluorescent lighting or just using lower wattage lights, will help reduce visually fueled temptations. Mirrors, especially in combination with bright lights, can pose problems for many people. Scrutinizing your skin inches from a mirror can reveal imperfections even for a person with healthy skin. Standing very close to regular mirrors is a step closer to taking action on perceived problems. However, when we take a step back (literally and figuratively) we can realize that the imperfections that may be noticeable with close scrutiny are hardly evident when viewed at a "normal" distance. If your bathroom poses a special challenge for you in this way, you would be wise to consider altering the way you relate to the mirror in this space. For example, practice standing at least an arm's length from the mirror when grooming, but not closer than that.

Another option available to some people is to temporarily cover the bathroom mirror. Taping wrapping paper or a poster over it could cover the mirror completely or partially. Try covering the top and leaving the bottom free. This will require you to bend down in order to see yourself in the remaining space. This less comfortable posture will encourage a quicker completion of your grooming tasks. You are less likely to get "stuck" in the mirror if you are bending down! Of course, such an approach must fit your lifestyle and circumstances.

Magnifying mirrors, especially illuminated ones, offer the worst of both worlds. If you pick your skin or pull your hair while using a magnifying mirror, you will be confronted with an unrealistic image that highlights and grotesquely enlarges imperfections. This can easily provoke binges of picking or pulling. Seriously consider whether your grooming needs truly require a magnifying device. Most people can function quite well without them. Removing the device is one simple environmental change that can make a big difference for some people attempting to manage their BFRB.

Tweezers, pins, needles, or any kind of implement used for grasping hair or skin, or for delving beneath the surface of the skin, also may be serving as "implements of destruction." Simply having those items readily available creates situations where the urge to pluck hair or pick at skin can go far beyond what was intended. In these cases, you must consider if you truly need these implements to be so readily accessible, especially near a mirror. If disposing of these items seems too extreme, consider putting them in a baggie filled with water and placing them in the freezer. If at some later time you truly need any of these items for legitimate purposes, the ice can easily be melted in a pan of water on the stove (*but don't put them in the microwave!*), or just let them melt at room temperature. This will provide you the time to use other measures in your plan to get through these situations, while the ice melts! Don't forget to refreeze them afterwards. If you are a hair puller who finds that normal depilation activities, such as plucking eyebrows or removing chin hairs, leads to episodes of hair pulling that go far beyond the original intent, a better alternative might be to get your grooming needs taken care of by a professional esthetician, beautician, or hair removal expert until you gain better control. If you suffer from a BFRB and it is within your financial means, we encourage you to consider these alternatives until you can safely manage these activities on your own. Others can improvise less costly interventions to address these grooming issues.

Create reminders: Another potentially helpful way to change the environment is by using reminders in locations where you are tempted to pick or pull. We have mentioned before that placing notes in places where you regularly engage in self-damaging activity can be useful. Appropriately placed notes can remind you to be aware of your environment, and to use your planned interventions within that environment. Placing brightly colored sticky notes on your television or computer can remind you to use your interventions before you settle in to watch a program or to check your emails. Visual cues can also encourage you to use multiple interventions simultaneously for extra protection against BFRB urges. Write down phrases such as "Use your finger bandages" or "Do you have your rubber fingertips on?" Seeing these *before* you start watching TV or *before* you begin brushing your hair can prompt you to use interventions that may mean the difference between success and disappointment. Prearranged cues serve as cognitive interventions that can help you to be forewarned, forearmed, and ready to fight temptation. If a written note is awkward in your living situation, a brightly colored blank sticky note can serve as a discrete reminder. You can be the only person who knows what the blank note means, but it can still serve to jog your memory to use appropriate interventions.

If you are more technologically inclined, try adding an alarm on your smart phone or smart watch as an auditory reminder for you to use your interventions. With the advent of apps (phone or computer applications), be on the lookout for BFRB apps that can help you in your program.

Hair pulling and skin picking do not have to be accepted as inevitable just because you have consistently succumbed to episodes of self-damage in situations that you find yourself in on a daily basis. Following some of the suggestions provided in this chapter can have a bigger impact on disruption of "business as usual" than you realize.

In the following example you will learn how one young mother became aware of the impact that her environment had on her skin picking. See how she makes changes in the Place domain that help her gain greater control over her problem.

Melissa's Story

Melissa regularly watches TV with her children early in the morning before they begin their day. On this day she leans back in her armchair, with her legs pulled close to her body and her bare feet within easy reach and tries to relax while her young daughters watch "Dora the Explorer" for the third time that day. Unconsciously, she rubs her hands together and immediately discovers dry, "sharp" pieces of skin around her cuticles and nails. She picks at each rough spot until she has removed as much of the dry skin as she can. Now she is totally focused on her skin and examines it closely, touching each cuticle with her fingertips to make sure the skin is as smooth as she can get it. "Dora" plays in the background and Melissa watches and continues to pick at the skin around her fingers, hardly aware of what she is doing. Her young daughter climbs onto her lap and says, "Mommy, you have a boo-boo! You have blood on your finger." Melinda gives a half-hearted excuse to her daughter and shoos her away because some dry, sharp edges of the skin on her feet have gotten her attention and she begins picking there too.

Stage 1: Building Her Awareness

In the scenario described above, Melissa's routine begins with a sedentary activity—she sits with free hands and easy access to her habitual picking sites. Not all routines that serve as situational triggers involve sitting still and having idle hands, however. In many cases, just the experience of entering a situation where picking or pulling has been part of the routine can be enough to trigger a BFRB episode. An appreciation of why this is so may be helpful. Here is Melissa's *Self-Monitoring Form*:

Self-Monitoring Form	
Where and What: In the family room, watching TV with kids.	
When: Thurs., 10/2	
Sitting in recliner.	S C A M (P)
Bored with kids' TV show.	S C (A) M P
Hands in lap rubbing cuticle; feet within easy reach.	S C A (M) P
Idle hands; rough skin.	(S) C A M P

What I did with the "product": Rubbed it between my fingers until it fell.

First aware of urge/behavior (0-4): 3	Amount that I picked or pulled (0-4): 3
0 = Entering situation, 4 = Mid to late in episode	0 = None, 4 = Extreme

TRY IT! Consider some rooms or locations where you tend to pick or pull. Make note of environmental elements that may be contributing your problem behaviors.

Stage 2: Planning and Preparation

Melissa became more aware of how her skin picking was influenced by her environment. Closely monitoring her activities in the family room as she watched TV with her children, she focused on the fact that she almost always sat in the reclining chair with her hands idle, initially resting in her lap, and with her feet bare much of the time. Being aware of these details enabled her to make some practical changes that greatly helped her to better manage her behavior. Then she looked at the *Master List of Interventions* and decided to make a few strategic changes in her behavior within this environment.

Melissa decided to change the spot where she regularly sat, this time joining her kids on the floor. She also decided to remain active during this time by folding laundry, going through mail, or engaging in other simple activities that occupied her hands.

She wanted to remind herself to make these changes, so she placed a yellow sticky note reminder on the head area of the recliner. It was blank, but to her it was a reminder—"Don't sit here!"

TRY IT!   Pick a place where picking or pulling is likely to occur. Consult the *Master List of Interventions* and circle the "Place" interventions that you might find helpful.

Stage 3: Putting Her Plan into Action

Now let's look at Melissa's *Action Plan* and see how she used her observations to generate new ideas about interventions.

Action Plan							
Situation (Location/Activity): Family room, watching TV with kids.							
When Started: Sun, April 22							
Interventions (Circle Relevant Domain Letters)	S	M	T	W	T	F	S
Problem: Idle hands. Intervention: Draw or give backrubs to kids. (S) C A (M) P		✓	✓		✓	✓	
Problem: Sitting in recliner. Intervention: Sit on floor. S C A M (P)		✓	✓	✓	✓	✓	✓
Problem: Sitting in recliner. Intervention: Reminder note to sit elsewhere. S (C) A M (P)							
Problem: Hands free to pick. Intervention: Fold laundry on floor. S C A (M)(P)		✓	✓		✓	✓	
Awareness (0-4) 0 = Entering setting 4 = Mid to late in episode	3	0	1	3	1	0	2
How much did I pick or pull? (0-4) 0 = None, 4 = Extreme	3	0	1	3	1	0	3
Comments: Remember to bring "busy hands" stuff into the TV room in the morning.							

When Melissa made these changes, not only did skin picking decline in that setting, but she had the added benefit of feeling closer to her children. She came to rely less on keeping her hands busy with chores and instead used them for physical interactions with her children. Idle hands became more loving hands.

ADDING "P" TO YOUR SCAMP TOOLBOX

In this chapter you learned how isolation and sedentary activities within certain environments could set the stage for hair pulling or skin picking. Many people enter these situations without forethought and therefore begin their BFRB routine without full awareness, or they find that, without their knowledge, features of the environment trigger irresistible temptations and urges. You learned how some specific techniques that alter the physical space and raise your awareness could enable you to gain control over your behaviors in problem environments. These techniques allow you to engage in your usual activities within the space, but in a way that will enable you to manage skin picking and hair pulling more effectively in your everyday places.

With the addition of "P," the Place (or environmental) domain, you now have all of the information necessary to fill your SCAMP toolbox with the necessary "tools." You have learned about a variety of techniques that are possible to use within the five SCAMP categories: Sensory, Cognitive, Affective, Motor, and Place.

With completion of the Place portion of our SCAMP formulation, you are now ready for the next step: the opportunity to develop your own truly comprehensive self-help plan. This plan will serve as a roadmap, guiding you through your journey of healing. Grab your SCAMP toolbox and start making ComB work for you!

CHAPTER 9

Putting It All Together

We are now coming full circle, back to the overall process that you first read about in chapter 3. At this point you have learned much about various aspects of your picking or pulling problem, including the five SCAMP domains, which has given you a framework for understanding the dynamics of your problem, the sequence of events within each BFRB episode, the array of interventions that can address the challenges of each domain, and some forms to guide your healing process.

In this chapter, we continue to build on the information from each chapter and are now in position to put it all together.

Getting this far, you know about each of the three stages of the ComB program: (1) Building Awareness, (2) Planning and Preparation, and (3) Putting Your Plan into Action. We hope you have jotted down notes and have completed some practice forms relevant to the previous chapters. You have already learned ways to manage each of the SCAMP domains as they apply to your circumstances and to your recovery. Trust that you are ready to combine the knowledge and skills that you have read about and that are now stored in your toolbox. This chapter will show you how to put them to good use.

> **TRY IT!** Gather together any notes you have previously jotted down. Print out a copy of the *Master List of Interventions* and multiple blank copies of the *Self-Monitoring Form* and the *Action Plan*, so that they are readily available, to ensure that you can move smoothly through the stages of your ComB program. (All of these are available on the New Harbinger website for this book: www.newharbinger.com/43645.)

The next step is to address the big picture and integrate everything that you have learned so far, using the familiar three-stage process. At this point you will actually go through the process of creating your own individualized plan.

STAGE 1: BUILDING YOUR AWARENESS

Choose a setting where you tend to pick or pull, and use your *Self-Monitoring Forms* to record some representative picking or pulling episodes. We suggest recording three days (one weekend day and two weekdays). It's best if you do that, but if this seems to be too much for you to do, please record at least one day.

Begin increasing your awareness by using your *Self-Monitoring Forms* to document one episode. Sue pulls her eyelashes and eyebrows in the bathroom while getting ready for the day. Here's an example of what her form might look like after completion.

Self-Monitoring Form	
Where and What: *In the bathroom getting ready for the day.*	
When: *Wed. 3/4*	
Privacy, hard to stop—no one to interrupt me.	S C A M **(P)**
Turned bright light on, got tweezers, leaned into the mirror, pulled prickly hairs.	S C A M **(P)**

Touched and saw prickly eyebrow hairs and lashes.	Ⓢ C A M P
Thought: Those hairs must go. I can fix it. I am alone and can pull	S Ⓒ A M P
Felt frustrated.	S C Ⓐ M P
Felt successful at removing unwanted hairs.	S C Ⓐ M P
Leaned close to mirror.	S C A Ⓜ P
Elbow bent, chin on hand close to eyes.	S C A Ⓜ P

What I did with the "product": Looked at the hairs briefly and then dropped them in the sink.

First aware of urge/behavior (0-4): 2	Amount that I picked or pulled (0-4): 3
0 = Entering situation, 4 = Mid to late in episode	0 = None, 4 = Extreme

Comments: I was not aware of a lot of this!

Using this example with Sue, you can see how occurrences in each domain are likely influencing the BFRB problem.

- **Sensory**

  Seeing and touching prickly eyelashes and eyebrow hairs

  Seeing eyelashes curled in the "wrong" direction

- **Cognitive**

  Thinking that the prickly eyelashes and eyebrow hairs don't belong there

  Thinking that I must remove the eyelashes curling in the wrong direction

  Thinking that I am alone and will not be interrupted

- **Affective**

  Feeling frustrated

  Feeling successful when removing hairs

- **Motor**

  Leaning toward mirror

  Chin resting on hand, elbow bent

- **Place**

  Bright lights in bathroom

  Easy access to tweezers

  Privacy

By reviewing this pulling episode, we can see that all of the domains can affect the behavior. Take time to review how each of these elements contributed to pulling. Interestingly, note that the feeling of being successful is not a trigger, but rather a consequence of the behavior that serves to maintain it. This can serve as a reminder to be aware not only of factors within domains that serve to *trigger* picking or pulling, but also to be aware of (and address the consequences of) effects that *maintain* these behaviors. In this example, Sue's feeling of being successful contributes to further pulling behaviors. In this case it might be useful to use a Cognitive intervention to remind her that pulling out hairs is self-damage— not a victory, but a failure of self-control. Perhaps she might memorize a statement like "The truth of the matter is that the result wasn't a success. This was a *failure* to maintain control and take care of myself," and then recite it each time she has pulled any hairs.

If feelings of accomplishment or success tend to follow incidents of picking or pulling, remind yourself of what they are—acts of self-damage that are no cause for celebration. Work to attain feelings of success when they are truly that—the times you actually beat back your BFRB. Those are real accomplishments! Find ways to make that a part of your program and you are well on your way to healing (and don't forget to include those techniques in your *Action Plan*).

> **TRY IT!**   Choose the setting you would like to start with. Then fill in your own *Self-Monitoring Form* as soon as possible after an episode in that location.

STAGE 2: PLANNING AND PREPARATION

During this stage of your plan, you will be selecting your interventions and preparing the environment.

Gather together your *Self-Monitoring Forms* and your *Master List of Interventions*, with its previously circled ideas, along with any additional ones you think you might need. Review the list and make any updates you would like (add new ones, or cross out interventions that you don't think you will use).

Now is the time to make note of the interventions you have chosen to use. We suggest choosing at least one intervention from three different domains.

Take the time and energy to set up your physical environment for success! Think about the supplies you will need, and at your earliest opportunity begin to gather them together. If you need something but don't have it, get it—buy it, borrow it, find a replacement for it—whatever! These might include items to use in order to satisfy a tactile sensory need, nail polish, cotton gloves, interesting items to handle, relaxation apps for your phone, and so on. Be creative and playful: enjoy yourself while engaging in this part of the process and remind yourself that your well-being is well worth it.

Place your supplies and materials where they are needed (a basket, box, or bowl may keep them from straying), then put them where they will be within easy reach from your usual spot in the setting you are focusing on. If you are in a public place, you may want to store your supplies in a drawer, or otherwise out of sight. You don't want to find yourself in a high-risk environment and have the urge to pick or pull, only to discover that supplies for your planned intervention are nowhere to be found. Even if they are in the same room, if they are not within arm's reach, standing up and walking across the room to get them may be just the lapse that your BFRB needs to gain the advantage.

If you would find it helpful, you may want to write a "To Do" list to assist in your preparation of interventions. Using Sue's example, here is what preparations for implementing her *Action Plan* might look like:

To Do

Unscrew all but one light bulb over the sink.

Replace the one light bulb with a lower wattage bulb.

Move tweezers out of the bathroom to the tool drawer.

Move makeup to bedroom near mirror.

Buy some fidget items and place them near toilet.

Put two sticky notes right in the middle of the mirror: "Leave the bathroom quickly!" and "Left alone, my eyelashes and eyebrows will grow soft and full!"

Get a textured sponge to wash my face.

Another form of preparation might be to get information about services that can potentially help you. These may include electrolysis, waxing, hairstyle changes, hair color changes, or appointments with physicians, dermatologists, estheticians, barbers, or hair stylists. These represent other ways of achieving desirable outcomes without engaging in self-damaging behaviors. If you have never used these kinds of services but want to learn more, get referrals from trusted sources, contact the providers with any questions you may have, and arrange for a consultation or phone conversation before getting treatment so you can get an idea about the risks, benefits, and costs.

> **TRY IT!** Collect materials; gather, borrow, or buy what you don't already have. Then put your supplies together in a very accessible location in the place you have chosen to win back.

STAGE 3: PUTTING YOUR PLAN INTO ACTION

Now you are on your way! Having done the preliminary preparation, you are ready to try out using your interventions for that one setting. As you know, you will use your *Action Plan* not only to describe your interventions and how they can help, but also as a way of tracking your progress. At this point you have available the full complement of ideas from all the domains at your disposal!

Here is Sue's *Action Plan* after seven days of using her plan:

Action Plan							
Situation (Location/Activity): *Getting ready for the day, bathroom.*							
When Started: *Wed., 3/17*							
Interventions (Circle Relevant Domain Letters)	S	M	T	W	T	F	S
Problem: *Bright lights.* Intervention: *Fewer light bulbs. One low-wattage bulb.* S C A M (P)	✓ ✓	✓ ✓	✓ ✓	✓ ✓	✓ ✓	✓ ✓	✓
Problem: *Too close to mirror while putting on makeup.* Intervention: *Move makeup to bedroom.* S C A M (P)	✓			✓			✓

Problem: Tweezers make it too easy to pull hairs. Intervention: Keep tweezers in toolbox. (S) C A M P			✓			✓
Problem: Close to mirror. Intervention: Stay arm's length from mirror. (S) C A (M) P			✓		✓	
Problem: Touching prickly hairs at mirror. Intervention: Use textured sponge, not hands, to wash face—keeps hands busy and make it harder to pull. (S) C A (M) P		✓	✓			
Problem: Feeling successful after removing hair. Intervention: If I pull hairs, recite my "Truth" statements. S C (A) M P		✓			✓	✓
Awareness (0-4) 0 = Entering setting 4 = Mid to late in episode	2	4	0	1	3	2	3
How much did I pick or pull? (0-4) 0 = None, 4 = Extreme	2	3	3	1	3	3	2
Comments: Was more aware but still had trouble, especially because I was still touching my eye area. I did better when I kept my tweezers in the tool drawer in the kitchen. I think I need more ideas and to be stricter with myself regarding my tweezers. I think I do need to try freezing them.							

Sue's plan has begun to make a difference, especially in increasing awareness. The interventions that she used had some degree of success, especially putting the makeup in the bedroom. As you can see above, over time she will learn which interventions are effective in each given setting (remember that some interventions might work well in some settings, but not in others). It seems that the biggest issue in this situation was that she kept the tweezers in the bathroom on most days. Now that she knows that this is a problem, she will modify her plan to address that.

TRY IT! Try out your initial plan using an *Action Plan* for a week. If you think you might benefit from modifications, make those changes and see if they help.

In this next step you can see that this is a process of trying and tweaking as needed. Sue's second-week *Action Plan* shows two additions that had a positive effect. See the changes, shown below in italics.

Action Plan Week 2							
Situation (Location/Activity): *Getting ready for the day, bathroom.*							
When Started: *Wed., 3/24*							
Interventions (Circle Relevant Domain Letters)	S	M	T	W	T	F	S
Problem: *Bright lights.* Intervention: *Fewer light bulbs. One low-wattage bulb.* S C A M (P)	✓	✓	✓	✓	✓	✓	✓
Problem: *Too close to large mirror while putting on makeup.* Intervention: *Move makeup to bedroom.* S C A M (P)	✓			✓			✓

	1	2	3	4	5	6	7
Problem: Belief that hairs will always be prickly. Intervention: Dispute belief—read or recite sticky notes aloud 3 times: "My eyelashes and eyebrows will grow in and soften up in time." S (C) A M P		✓	✓				
Problem: Tweezers make it too easy to pull hairs. Intervention: Keep tweezers in toolbox. (S) C A M (P)	✓			✓			✓
Problem: Feeling successful after removing hair. Recited the "Truth" statement and didn't feel so successful. S C (A) M P	✓		✓	✓		✓	
Problem: Bent elbows, resting head on hands. Intervention: Wear elbow brace. S C A (M) P	✓		✓	✓	✓	✓	✓
Problem: Touching prickly hairs at mirror. Intervention: Use textured sponge and wash face to keep hands busy and make it harder to pull. (S) C A (M) P			✓	✓			
Awareness (0-4) 0 = Entering setting 4 = Mid to late in episode	2	2	1	0	3	2	1
How much did I pick or pull? (0-4) 0 = None, 4 = Extreme	1	3	1	1	3	2	1

> **Comments:** *Forced myself to put tweezers in toolbox, added the elbow brace. I also added using coping statements. I liked them! I'm feeling more in control now!*

You can see from the scores, as well as from the comments and changes that were made on the second week, that the additions strengthened the plan and gave Sue a boost.

> **TRY IT!** Go ahead and work with your own revised plan for a week. (If you didn't need to revise it, continue with the same one.) At the end of that time, again assess your progress and tweak anything that needs adjusting. If you run into problems, continue making needed changes until the combination of interventions works in your favor.

WHAT TO DO IF YOU GET STUCK

As is the case with many others who are working hard to overcome their BFRB, you might not make progress as quickly or easily as you had hoped. That, as many have found, doesn't mean you won't ultimately be successful. But of course you won't know that if you give up too easily.

If you are struggling at any point in your program, refocus on adjusting your plan. You may well discover that small adjustments over time will result in the right formula for success. For instance, if you fail to use the combination of interventions that you planned to in drawing up your *Action Plan*, determine what extra measures you might take the next time you enter that situation. Be better prepared.

A change as simple as moving your supplies closer to where you are sitting so that they are easier to access, or putting a well-placed reminder note in a strategic place, might be just the small change that puts you back on track.

If more than a few weeks go by without making much progress on the first location, despite modifications, choose another setting to work on instead—perhaps one where the urges don't feel quite as strong, or one that doesn't have as long a history for picking or pulling as the first one did.

Working on a different setting might provide you with the opportunity for greater control, a battle won, and feelings of success. Each success will provide you with the confidence to move forward. At a later time you can go back and tackle the original setting that proved so difficult to manage. As is often the case, success breeds success.

OTHER SETTINGS

Once you have made satisfactory progress and established your new routine in one location, begin to add other settings to your plan, using the same process and forms as you did previously. Adding about two settings per week is probably manageable, but one per week is certainly good enough, so find your own pace. Ultimately, you will want to include all of the settings where you are vulnerable as you win back your freedom from pulling or picking. Remember that when you add each new location you will need to go through the same three stages as before, but because you are gaining more experience each day, you may find that you move through them more quickly.

GENERAL GUIDELINES AS YOU MOVE FORWARD

Pace Yourself

The *Self-Monitoring Form* you wrote up for the first location that you tackled provided you with new and useful information; those you complete for the additional settings will probably do the same.

As you continue to make progress, you will most likely have workable plans for all of your problem settings within a month or so, but remember that you should find your own pace. The process will allow you to create an effective and uniquely individualized plan; indeed, this is the hallmark of the ComB program.

If you move methodically from one location to the next, expect to be better prepared for each new opportunity to increase your knowledge and skills. Because the ComB method is based on learning, each success will remind you of your newfound abilities, and any bumps along the road will be increasingly well managed because you can use the challenges as learning opportunities. If you remain dedicated to the process, then the challenges, though they may not be exactly welcome, will not prevent you from continuing on your journey.

You Don't Have to Reinvent the Wheel

As you move forward addressing each setting, you will notice that certain aspects of your problem reappear in a variety of settings. This means that you are likely to find that the same interventions you find useful in one setting can be used in more than one location, so you don't have to start from scratch with each setting. Some of these (such as using fiddle toys or hand lotion) can actually provide benefits in more than one domain. For instance, fiddle toys or worry beads can serve motor, sensory, and even affective functions. The benefits of applying nail polish while watching TV cut across the Sensory, Motor, and Place domains. In fact, you may find that a few interventions are so versatile and reliable that they will be able to serve you in many situations so effectively that they will become your fallback interventions. Finally, remember that many interventions weaken the chain of events from which your BFRB derives its power. In other words, *as you gain strength, your BFRB grows weaker.*

Review Your Plan and Modify as Needed

We hope that you will enjoy early success, and that you will celebrate every improvement, big and small. As you head into the weeks ahead and continue using your program, you should begin to enjoy the fruits of your efforts. The vision of a life where you are not at the mercy of your picking or pulling is why you have gotten this far in this book. As your efforts pay off, you will become more certain that a life no longer spoiled by pulling or picking is a realistic and attainable goal.

We recognize that this process may not be an easy one, and that at times you might feel discouraged. But if you encounter unforeseen challenges and disappointments, we urge you to see them as instructive, for they often reveal weaknesses in your plan that are correctable. Corrective adjustments that you make in your plan can have a cascading effect: successfully problem-solving in one situation will maximize your chances of success in others. This process offers almost limitless opportunities to brainstorm and problem-solve whatever problems are encountered in making your program work for you. If you maintain a thoughtful, flexible, and creative problem-solving approach throughout—well, let's just see how good it can get!

IT PAYS TO BE PATIENT AND PERSISTENT!

Over the years, we have found that when people feel stuck, answering the following questions can jump-start the process:

- Are my supplies easily available and within arm's reach?

- Am I using my chosen interventions each time I am in problematic locations?

- Am I using at least three interventions in each setting?

- Am I using my interventions *as soon as* I settle into the space (before I get an urge, look in a mirror, or touch the target area)?

If you answered "no" to any of the above questions, they can point to what you can do to strengthen your plan. If you need some additional tips, try these ideas:

- Consider adding one or two interventions within the same domain, or swapping out interventions that don't seem to "click" for others that may prove more helpful.

- Add one or two interventions from a domain that you haven't included yet.

- If you have worked with a combination of interventions for a few weeks and made appropriate adjustments only to discover that your plan is still not giving you the results you want, go back and examine the information on your *Self-Monitoring Form* to discover new clues, so you can figure out what adjustments you might make in your plan.

We encourage you to think of this process as an opportunity for honing your creativity and problem-solving abilities. At some point you might even want to revisit some of the interventions that you tried before you started reading this book. You may be surprised to find that they are more useful now that they are used in combination with those from other domains. There is strength in numbers! Be creative—be playful—be resourceful.

CONCLUSION

You may have noticed that in developing your behavior management plan for your BFRB, you have drawn upon your capacity for flexibility, patience, persistence, and self-compassion. These qualities will help you make your plan a success. As an extra bonus, these are also skills for living, skills that can be important for life beyond your current focus on your BFRB. Indeed, we hope this experience will open your world to new information, new ideas, and new discoveries.

PART 3

Moving on from Your Body-Focused Repetitive Behaviors

CHAPTER 10

Maintaining and Troubleshooting Your Plan

As you look ahead to the future and anticipate greater control over picking or pulling, what are your expectations about how this process will play out and how it will impact your life? We believe that it will benefit you by allowing you to experience a wide range of emotions as your life changes. Many of them will be positive, including hope, excitement, happiness, and determination. Some of them will be more challenging, including moments of frustration and disappointment.

What you may not have thought as much about is that the experience of working toward your recovery will be part of the broader fabric of your life. In fact, it might surprise you to realize that this work you are doing might contribute to a way of living that is more respectful of your body, your heart, and your mind. *We want you to take care of yourself as a whole person, not just as a person with a BFRB problem.* However, you are reading this book for a reason, and that reason is that you are struggling with skin picking or hair pulling. So we will continue to focus on that, but keep in mind that whatever we say about your recovery from skin picking or hair pulling may well have a much greater application for you in the bigger picture.

You have received guidance and support as you have gone through the ComB program described in this book. In this process, you have learned about and practiced developing your plan and using interventions tailored to your unique needs, with the goal of freeing yourself from a behavior pattern that has worked against your happiness and well-being. We hope that your early efforts have been rewarding and given you more hope and confidence in yourself, not only regarding your BFRB but maybe with some other areas of your life as well.

But we also are aware that you will probably need to practice a certain amount of vigilance, self-discipline, and creative problem-solving during this process, especially during the earliest stages. And we want to remind you that it is possible that you will want to continue using some elements of the ComB program at certain times even once your BFRB is under control. Keeping this in mind can help save you from becoming discouraged by the inevitable disappointments you will encounter.

In this chapter we will try to answer some questions you may have that are directly related to your ComB plan, and ones that have implications for other areas of your life as well: How can I manage bumps in the road? As I make progress, when and how can I phase back?

What will my life be like without picking or pulling?

WHAT ABOUT BUMPS IN THE ROAD?

We hope that your plan reduces your urges and enables you to gain better control of your picking or pulling in most settings. The good news is that you have taken the time to learn and practice new skills. If you have followed the steps of the ComB program, it is likely that you are already seeing the fruits of your labor. Perhaps you are also looking forward to the possibility of relief from your problem, and to a well-deserved new experience of life.

But old, familiar habits have a way of slipping in through the back door, so expect that at times you may consciously or unconsciously be caught unprepared. Let's return to an example based on the exercise you did in chapter 9 ("Putting It All Together"). You might remember the scenario where one person's danger zone was in the bathroom, sitting on the toilet, touching short, sharp eyelash and eyebrow hairs, then using tweezers while looking in the mirror.

Imagine yourself in that person's place. Your *Action Plan* for the bathroom was the following:

- Place: Move makeup from the bathroom to the bedroom, where there is less privacy and dimmer lighting.

- Place: Move tweezers to the tool drawer.

- Cognitive: Write sticky notes: "My lashes and eyebrows will grow in and soften over time," to correct misconceptions, and put them on the mirror.

- Motor: Use an elbow brace and hand lotion to keep my hands busy and increase awareness.

Now let's fast-forward to a month later. Let's say that your plan worked well enough for a while, but you didn't like using the lotion, so you stopped using it, and the elbow brace is no longer enough to reliably stop your hands from accessing your eye area. It is also hard to get on and take off, so you don't usually use it.

On this particular day, you are sitting on the toilet, and your fingertips have made contact with the prickly hairs that you're prone to pull. This sensation bothers you so much you tell yourself that you can't stand it—they just have to go. So after using the toilet you retrieve your tweezers from the tool drawer, return to the bathroom, and pull the bothersome hairs out with the help of the bathroom mirror. This is the third time in two weeks that this has happened, and you are now beginning to get very discouraged. So you take a look at your *Action Plan* and think about what you might need to do to improve the plan.

TRY IT! What would you change on your *Action Plan* if you were in that situation? Would you omit anything? What might you add, and why? If you have an actual situation that is similar, take a look at your *Action Plan* and your *Master List of Interventions* and write some ways that you could strengthen your plan.

The above is a thought experiment—a simulation of something you might actually do when you have to solve a recurrent problem so you can make progress at a faster pace. Analyzing and reworking your plan, adding or modifying your interventions until they suit your needs, and being diligent about recording your progress will help you find your way when you feel stuck. In the above scenario, the "Motor" interventions were not working well enough during the first part of the episode—while on the toilet. Since touching the eye area while on the toilet occurs early in the chain of events, it is especially helpful to have effective interventions at that point in time.

The good news is that the ComB method provides you with many options. You can go to the "Motor" section of your *Master List of Interventions*. Remember that this domain focuses on increasing awareness by blocking access to the picking or pulling site, or by otherwise interfering with contact between fingertips and the eye area and keeping hands busy with activity that does not promote picking or pulling. In this situation you would want to find one or more interventions that could serve these functions. You might decide to abandon the elbow brace altogether for now. Instead, you will wear reading glasses while sitting on the toilet and then, after putting on some hand lotion, you will play with some smooth stones or fiddle toys that you might find even more interesting when your hands are slippery with lotion. After toileting you might try setting a timer and trying to "beat the clock" so that you just have time to wash your face and brush your teeth by the time it goes off. So now you have a new set of interventions and this is what your "To Do" list might look like (new ideas are in *italics*):

- Place: Move my makeup from the bathroom to the bedroom, where there is less privacy and dimmer lighting, *and set a timer for 3 minutes as soon as I get off of the toilet—just enough time to brush my teeth and wash my face.*

- Place: Move tweezers to the tool drawer.

- Cognitive: Write sticky notes: "My lashes and eyebrows will grow in and soften over time," and put them on the mirror to correct misconceptions. (Putting them on the mirror also partially blocks view of the mirror—an intervention that operates in both the Sensory and Place domains.)

- Motor: *Wear glasses and play with fiddle toys when on toilet to increase awareness, keep my hands away from eye area, and keep my hands and fingers busy.*

Here you can see that although you might have been frustrated, you took the challenge and thought of ideas that might better meet your needs. Apply this kind of problem-solving technique when your plan isn't working as well as it should.

PHASING BACK WHEN YOU ARE READY

When you have achieved a certain level of success in a given setting, for several weeks to several months, you might be able to reduce your dependence on interventions if you can do so in a careful, gradual, and systematic way to minimize your risk of a setback.

Throughout this book you have learned ways to take care of your body and to look out for your nervous system's needs, using a combination of interventions that work together. When the time is right for you, carefully assess your daily use of these measures and evaluate how effective they are currently. Now may be the time to explore the possibility of reducing your reliance on interventions. Begin by choosing an intervention from the ones that you have been using. It should be one that you don't think is necessary for your continued success, and therefore one that may not be necessary at this time.

Then consider decreasing its use in a specific time, location, and activity where your problem seems well controlled. For example, you may determine that wearing bandages on your fingertips is less necessary at work due to other helpful changes you have made, like leaving your office door open more often, having interesting desk "toys" to reach for when the need arises, and taking occasional "stand up and move" breaks when working at your desk.

You might experiment with not wearing fingertip bandages at work for one day and see what happens. You may find that the absence of finger bandages does not result in increased urges or actual picking or pulling. If that is the case, you may consider going without them the next day as well, and so on, until you are confident that you don't need them anymore in those circumstances. Still, you might want to keep a few in your desk drawer in case they are needed again at some point.

Eventually, moving deeply into the ComB method, you may find that the interventions that were necessary earlier in your program will be replaced with ordinary activities of daily life. But be wise about this: Even after replacement measures have been introduced, new motor habits have not yet been firmly established. This means that your replacement behaviors will need to be supported by other means until your hands have been retrained to keep away from your picking and pulling sites. If all goes well, the time you used to spend picking or pulling can now be spent on enjoyable and healthy alternatives, such as leisure time or time spent with family or friends.

Taking up hobbies that can keep you (and your hands) busy and that can replace the temporary interventions (like gloves, for example) might be very useful—and fun. Some examples are gardening, cooking, needlepoint, doing crossword puzzles, and coloring in adult coloring books.

Often, new routines that replace the function that picking or pulling previously served are at the top of the list of interventions that can become beneficially woven into daily life. These include positive self-care and wellness activities, and also physical activities, such as walking, yoga, and dancing. Even in less notable ways, we hope that you will continue to respond to your body's needs by stimulating and soothing your senses with interesting items to "fidget" with, chew, listen to, smell, suck on, or eat.

Even now, you can begin to enjoy the sensations of a loofa sponge against your skin in a warm shower, establish healthful and relaxing hair-care and skin-care routines, get regular exercise, meditate, and practice other activities that relax or invigorate your body and your mind. Indulge in pleasurable activities or just reconnect with friends, relatives, or acquaintances. There are many more possibilities; these are just a few, and we are confident that you can come up with even more that fit your life perfectly, even as you are still working with this program!

MORE BUMPS IN THE ROAD

Sometimes, when we have made changes in our life that are good for us, like getting more exercise, eating healthier foods, or keeping a budget, we may "fall off the wagon." Who hasn't had that experience? As this relates to BFRBs, you can think of such lapses as *slips*—the occasional, limited reappearance of picking or pulling after a period of remission. A more serious lapse might be termed a *setback* (a more significant recurrence of picking or pulling in limited locations) or a *relapse* when you have made progress but then reverted to BFRB levels as bad or worse than they were before you started using the ComB method.

Most experts agree that, due to the nature of BFRBs, occasional slips after achieving some degree of success are an almost inevitable fact of life, and our clinical experience backs this up. We wish this wouldn't happen to you, but honestly, it probably will—so we want you to be prepared!

WHAT CAUSES SLIPS, BACKSLIDES, AND RELAPSES?

When slips occur after you have been making progress for a number of days, weeks, or even months, they may seem to have come from out of the blue. Upon close examination, however, a few common features can be identified that typically play important roles in these unwanted events. Here are some points to consider if you have experienced a setback.

Is your plan strong enough? You might think that your plan is "good enough" even if your progress is minimal. Don't settle for this! If you haven't made substantial progress in a given setting within a week or two, your enthusiasm for the plan may peter out, and that's when slips (or worse) can occur and set you back more than you bargained for. Instead, think of slips as signals to go back to the self-monitoring "drawing board." Study and rework the two other stages of treatment and keep tweaking your plan until it serves you well.

Life events. Certain significant experiences can derail efforts that require predictability, time, energy, and focus—efforts such as working toward BFRB recovery. Life and family transitions and other significant changes (even the happiest ones) often involve changes in locations or schedules, or a shift in your relationships. Other situations, such as having a strong emotional reaction to an event, a physical illness, or a major problem with family, school, or work, can have similar effects. These situations can create stress, distractions, and an increase in demands on your time, energy, and emotional reserves, any of which can leave you vulnerable to slips or setbacks. Are you expecting any transitions in the near future, such as a change in job, a marriage, a baby, a move, or a return to school? Be aware that even wonderful, happy life changes like getting married, having a new baby, or getting a promotion can pose challenges to your program.

When you get caught off guard. After weeks or even months of success, some people prematurely or abruptly stop engaging in self-monitoring, stop documenting the use of specific interventions in their *Action Plan*, or abandon the overall state of vigilance that led to their success. Such slips are reminders that when you are doing well and don't think your plan is needed anymore, it is important to wean yourself off of them in a gradual and systematic way. In addition, you will want to keep the supplies that have been useful so you can return to them if you have to.

Don't let slips slip by you. Prevent a slip from becoming a relapse by anticipating potential times of vulnerability, remembering that you now have a plan that can be continually adjusted to keep your program working for you. Plan ahead to move quickly and firmly to minimize the negative impact of any slips that may occur. Another way to look at slips is to see them as learning opportunities, for it will be the challenging times that will tell you where your plan is weak so you can make it stronger.

We tell people that they are never back to square one once they have worked with the ComB program. After all, the approach is based on helping you and others learn new ways of problem-solving. No lapse or setback can deprive you of the knowledge you have gained. Use it as an opportunity to move forward, better prepared than ever to make further progress.

CREATING A NEW NORMAL

The final step in the ComB program is to look ahead to your future and a "new normal." This will be comprised of healthy daily routines and new ways of engaging in life. Each new day can provide novel ways to address the challenges that lie ahead and to meet situations where you can use the knowledge and experiences you have gained to your advantage and for your well-being. Your life story will certainly look different from every other person's because it is your unique creation.

Even now you can take some time to evaluate the recommendations that have been meaningful to you up to this point in this book. Practice of the ComB program has the capability of ensuring a successful reduction or a total elimination of picking or pulling over the longer term. Some of the changes you have made may be of the bigger sort, such as fitting in exercise several times each week. Other changes may be smaller, such as keeping your fiddle toys close by in the right situations. Big or small, we hope that each of these changes in your life supports your efforts to care for yourself in positive, productive ways as well as to enhance your overall sense of well-being. This is your new normal. We have a feeling that you have been longing to participate in the world with newfound enthusiasm and confidence, and that it is not just wishful thinking, but a snapshot of your future.

WHAT TO DO WHEN SELF-HELP IS NOT ENOUGH

We truly hope that when you reach this point in the program you have made significant progress and that your future looks promising. We recognize, however, that you might not have yet attained the degree of control over your BFRB that you had hoped for. What can be done when your self-help program has simply not been effective enough for you to feel satisfied with your efforts to overcome these very formidable problems? If you are able, you may consider entering therapy with a trained professional to help guide you through this process. The TLC Foundation (bfrb.org) has a list of professionals throughout the country who have training and experience treating BFRBs. For some, this may be an excellent direction. For others, seeking professional assistance may be prohibitively expensive or not feasible for other reasons. What then? You may consider bringing this book to a trusted family member, friend, confidant, clergy, or other person to help you work with this program. Consider reaching out to an online BFRB support group, or an in-person support group if an active one is available in your community. Sometimes, having someone provide support through this process can be enormously helpful.

You may also need time to reflect on your experiences as you have gone through this book—time to digest what you have learned; time to reorganize yourself and get ready to embark on the your next phase; time to rally your resources and support.

This is a complicated process and one that may require more than one attempt. Be open to acknowledging your feelings and experience, and most importantly, be gentle with yourself in accepting that your journey toward recovery is not yet complete. We are aware of many individuals whose success in overcoming pulling and picking required a second or third sincere effort.

In the meantime, remember that your BFRB does not, and never will, define you. Your value lies in the three-dimensional person who happens to pull her hair or pick his skin. Take full pride in who you are as a person, and when you are ready, try again. Remember that having gone through this book has resulted in enormous amounts of learning about your problem, and about your own inner strengths and capabilities.

CHAPTER 11

Healthy Skin, Healthy Hair, Healthy Life

Thus far in this book you have spent time focusing on your own unique behavior patterns and how to help manage them. Let's shift gears for a moment so you can gain information about hair and skin with implications regarding your BFRB and your recovery, and how they fit into the larger picture of a cultivating a healthy life style.

THE IMPORTANCE OF SKIN AND HAIR

A miracle of evolution, the organ system technically called the "integumentary" system (from a Latin word meaning "to cover") consists of your skin, hair, and nails. It also includes "exocrine glands" within the skin's matrix, which produce sweat, oil, and wax. This system provides a waterproof, insulating "envelope" on the exterior of your body to keep it from drying out, being invaded by germs and toxins, or becoming overheated or too cold. It also serves a cleansing function by releasing waste products. As a part of the sensory system, the skin signals danger in the form of pain. Furthermore, your skin is a source of sensual pleasure, connection with others, and emotional comfort. As if all of this weren't enough, your skin also has a nutritional function, converting sunlight into Vitamin D. You could live without any number of your organs or body parts, but you could not survive without your skin.

Your hair isn't a necessity for life, but it still has important roles beyond appearance. While body hair doesn't have as much of an insulation function in humans as it does in many other mammals, head hair provides warmth in cold weather, as any bald person can tell you. Your eyebrows keep water and perspiration from dripping into your eyes, while your sensitive eyelashes detect foreign particles and aid the blink reflex in preventing foreign bodies from getting into your eyes. Pubic hair protects the genital area in some ways, and also contributes to sexual arousal.

An important point of information for people with BFRBs is that your skin has millions of pores. These pores are the portals between the outside world and the interior of the body, releasing oils, sweat, and toxins, as well as being the point of exit for every hair on your body. Pores are also the point of entry into the body for both beneficial and harmful substances: topical medicines, bacteria, and other sources of infections or irritation.

WHEN BFRB PROBLEMS ARISE

Most of us take the health of our hair and skin for granted. But they can become the source of much physical and emotional pain when problems arise. Nowhere is this more true than in the case of BFRBs. Your picking or pulling problem may have begun innocently enough, such as when an unexpected sensation of pleasure or relief from discomfort occurred when you removed a stray hair, a pimple, or ingrown hair. In that way, BFRBs can sneak up on people who are just trying to improve their appearance or to deal with discomfort. One thing leads to another, and what began as a brief action inadvertently expands, irritating or doing damage to the area. The skin wants to heal, so it may protect itself by producing thickened or calloused tissues, or even scarring, but these can be unsightly and interfere with the ability of pores in that area to do their job. This can create even more problems, with hairs or substances that typically exit through the pores being trapped beneath the surface of the skin. Over a period of months or years, the upper layers of skin in that area may become compromised, exposing the lower layers of the skin to possible infections and other problems. All that being said, the resilience of the body is amazing. Even many people who have picked or pulled for long periods of time have found that, when they learned techniques to help them resist engaging in excessive grooming and begin to support the natural healing process through healthy grooming, their skin and hair responded better than they could have imagined.

We hope you find the information in this chapter helpful in your efforts to regain and maintain the healthy skin and hair that you seek, and that you will also consider how the recommendations might fit into the bigger picture of a healthier and happier you.

THE ANATOMY OF SKIN, HAIR, AND NAILS

Your skin consists of several layers, each with its own complexity, and sublayers, each of which has a role to play in protecting and fostering your health. Your hairs and nails are specialized skin cells that offer added protection to the body, as well as other useful functions that affect your life in many ways.

Your Skin

The "fatty" innermost layer connects with underlying nerve cells, fatty tissue, and blood and lymph vessels. These are living cells that support and transport essentials to and from the interior of your body. The middle layer (the derma) is made up of strong, elastic connective tissue, glands that produce oils and sweat, and tiny capillaries that transport oxygen and other nutrients to the area while taking up toxins for removal from the body. The outer layer, the epidermis, has several layers of its own. The bottom layers generate living skin cells that are pushed toward the surface as new cells are formed below. As those older cells move to the surface, they lose access to their sources of nourishment—and there they complete their life cycle and die. Near the surface of the skin the dead cells form an interlocked covering, which protects the living layers of skin below. Over time, the dead skin cells are shed—millions every day—and are replenished from within. The whole process takes thirty-five to forty-five days.

When pores of the epidermis become clogged as a result of waxy build-up, makeup, dirt, bacteria, or other substances, whiteheads, blackheads, or other blemishes can result. It can be hard to resist the impulse to remove these. But even so, many people are able to do it carefully, with clean hands, using a technique their dermatologist taught them, along with understanding the importance of waiting until the blemish has "come to a head." However, given your picking or pulling problems, it may be very hard for you to wait, to take hygienic precautions, or to resist going deeper. You can know when you have not waited long enough or that you have gone too far when blood or clear fluid appears, because at that point you have gone below the epidermis. These are signs that you have caused damage to your skin and made it vulnerable to discoloration, rawness, and infections. In addition, the healing process often involves the creation of scabs or toughened skin, both of which are common targets for scraping or scratching, which in turn, further damages the skin.

Your Hair

Within the derma resides the base of the hair follicle, a tiny sheath that generates the hair bulb from which the hair shafts develop. Each follicle has a tiny gland that produces sebum, a waxy substance that moistens the hair shaft. As new cells are created, the cells become the hair shaft that gets pushed upwards and then emerges through the pore. The length and thickness of the shaft grow over a period of months or years, depending on the location and type of hair. When the root has completed its life cycle (from several months to several years, depending on where it is located on the body), it dies and the hair is shed. The hair shaft itself does not consist of living cells, which is why it doesn't hurt when you get your hair cut. It is also the reason why, when you brush your hair and some hairs come out, what are removed are the hairs with roots that are no longer living, which is why they don't have fat roots and their removal doesn't hurt.

When you pull out a hair, depending on where it is in its life cycle, the root may still have living cells and contact with sensory nerves and a blood supply. This is why it can hurt a bit upon extraction, and the root may look "fat" and moist, and might even have a drop of blood on the end. Pulling out a hair with a "live bulb" doesn't mean that the hair won't grow back. This is because you haven't removed the follicle, the part that remains in the skin that generates new hair bulbs from which the hair shafts grow. Some people who pull hairs report pleasurable sensations experienced at the moment of hair extraction. Others report neutral sensations or even pain upon extraction, but when they examine the hair and see a large bulb or a spot of blood on the end of the root, they may experience a rewarding feeling.

Your Nails and Cuticles

Nails, too, are initially formed by living layers of cells below the surface. Nail cells are created in the nail "bed" under the cuticles. The cells migrate outward to the surface, and eventually serve their purpose as nonliving cells that protect the living cells beneath. Fingernails, with the help of our opposable human thumb, are precision tools that can grasp and manipulate many tiny things, enabling people to draw, use the computer, and do hand sewing. But these same abilities are the reason that you are easily able to engage in your BFRB, either by using your fingers or by employing implements such as tweezers or needles.

The hard surfaces of both fingernails and toenails are composed of dead cells. These parts of the body need to be tough in order to protect your fingers or toes. But because they are firmly attached to living skin, cutting (or biting, or picking) them too short can create pain and bleeding. The cuticles create the boundary between the skin and the nails. This border of thick skin can be gently trimmed or pushed back to avoid rough ridges or jagged edges. However, when you trim too much (or use your teeth to pull off the rough edges), you can accidentally cut or pull off the adjacent living tissues, which in turn can cause the body to create a protective thickening of the skin, creating that vicious cycle we have discussed previously.

WHEN GROOMING GETS OUT OF CONTROL

Your skin and hair need to be cared for, nourished, and hydrated as part of a healthy grooming regime. Normal grooming may include using cleansing, moisturizing, or gentle exfoliation to remove the top layer of dead skin, being careful to avoid harsh chemicals or other products that scrape or harm the skin. In the general population, modifying or removing stray or bothersome hairs, or occasionally picking at scabs or dry skin a bit prematurely, is not uncommon, as is careful trimming or removal of errant hairs by using scissors, depilatory cream, a razor, or tweezers. In most cases, though, these grooming techniques do not harm the skin, hair, or nails. But when people go too far and experience pain or other signs of damage, the healthy response is to not repeat the process. At its core, the challenge for you is to be able to keep grooming within reasonable bounds.

The underlying vulnerability that leads some people to develop a BFRB is not well understood. There is some evidence that there may be genetic predispositions or other biological features that contribute to acquiring these problems. Regardless of the underlying causes, what triggers initial episodes is varied. For some people, irritants (such as poison ivy or bug bites) can lead to pulling, scratching, rubbing, or scraping. While some people may recall, or think they recall, what prompted their first experience of picking or pulling, for most people that information is unavailable. Yet we know that the initial experience of these activities must have delivered some sort of "payoff" for some people, because the practice continued as a BFRB that took on a life of its own.

Meanwhile, the body's automatic response is to heal and protect, and that can create rough areas, callouses, scabs, lesions, new-growth hairs, and irregular and malformed hairs. Then these self-induced changes become new triggers for even more picking or pulling. In addition, over time the hands may be drawn by subtle sensations from the affected areas, which can draw further attention to those spots and can lead to more BFRB activity.

Usually, the more you pick or pull, the more damage is created. That means it will take that much longer for the skin to heal or for the normal regrowth of hair to take place. For instance, you may search for and pick off scabs because they are annoying to look at or unpleasant to the touch. In doing so you may think that this will accelerate the healing process. The reality is that if you had waited, the scabs would have eventually shrunk and fallen off on their own when the skin below was sufficiently healed. Now the skin has to form a new scab and healing will take longer.

If you believe that pulling out hairs that have undesirable features (for instance, too coarse, too curly, the "wrong" color; or short, prickly hairs that are just growing in) will allow more desirable hairs to grow in their place, you're just plain wrong. However, if you repeatedly pull hair from the same follicle, it may go into temporary shock or even become permanently damaged. In either case, the hairs it generates may, at least for a time, become distorted in color, texture, or shape—or the follicles may be rendered incapable of producing any more hairs at all. Fortunately, follicles tend to be resilient and hair has natural variations in texture and color. Prickly new hairs almost always soften as they get longer. If you can be patient, given enough time, follicles will usually regain health when the damage caused by pulling is halted, and the new growth will likely regain its former look and feel.

DEALING WITH DAMAGED SKIN OR HAIR

You are probably experiencing some unfortunate physical consequences of skin picking or hair pulling. As mentioned above, skin that is damaged by picking can form scabs, callouses, or scars—all as natural reactions to protect the skin. If you have medical problems such as eczema, flare-ups of your condition can make it even harder to tolerate waiting or resisting the temptation to scratch or remove irritated skin. It is common for people to attempt to "pop" their pimples, and squeeze their skin in the hopes of promoting healing. Many of these individuals unintentionally create bruising, bleeding, swelling, and discoloration, among other indications of damage. Furthermore, such activities can drive minor infections deeper into the skin, causing more serious medical issues. The distress that results from the realization that more damage has been done can lead to even more desperate efforts to "correct" the problems, resulting in yet more rough, bruised scabbed, calloused, scarred, and discolored skin.

Likewise, as mentioned earlier, hair pulling can lead to greater problems such as ingrown hairs and damaged hair follicles, which may result in a thickened or otherwise altered texture or color of the hair. This may in turn promote intensified pulling to locate and eliminate such hairs. Ingrown hairs, which can occur anywhere on the body, present special problems. If you pierce the skin with tweezers or pins to remove the embedded hair, you can damage both the skin and the hair follicle. Over time, these practices can produce multiple problems, such as scarring or thickening of the skin, making ingrown hairs more likely. Infections on the scalp or skin in other areas can slow or prevent the very healing that would eventually produce the healthy skin and hair that you long for.

SKIN AND HAIR PRODUCTS

During your process of recovery, consider using some skin care products to exfoliate, balance the skin's chemistry, and replenish moisture and nutrients that are lost in the wear and tear of daily life. Select products that are tailored to your skin type, your age, and whether or not you have any special health considerations. These requirements will change over time because there are natural changes to skin and hair as we get older: Hair will become thinner and skin wrinkles will develop as the natural lubricants and hormones of youth begin to diminish.

You don't have to spend a fortune on products that advertise heavily and that make claims that their products are miracle cures, and that their products alone will transform the lives of their users. Instead, you can buy reasonably priced products from local drug stores. Look for those that have been developed or recommended by dermatologists, that are nonirritating, that include natural ingredients (including vitamins), and that are "noncomedogenic" (designed not to clog pores). Wearing sunscreen faithfully is one of the best things you can do to protect your skin from damaging UVA and UVB rays, which can cause early skin aging and contribute to skin cancer. The American Academy of Dermatology Association has an excellent website that can answer any questions you may have about sunscreen (see the "Resources and References" section at the end of this book for contact information).

HEALTHY SKIN AND HAIR FROM THE INSIDE OUT

Whether you are dealing with healthy skin or problem skin, it is wise to develop an attitude of moderation, self-respect, and tender loving care. Try to make your BFRB recovery program part of a self-care regime that can replace damaging grooming activities. The regime should include exfoliating, strengthening, hydrating, nourishing, and protecting your skin and hair. But there's more: it turns out that when you are taking care of your body as a whole, you will also reap benefits that can support your recovery from your HPD or SPD. As you read the following passages on wellness, keep in mind how they may also help you engage in activities that will then benefit your efforts to end skin and hair problems. You might even recognize some SCAMP domains and interventions among these recommendations.

Healthy Eating Habits

New information is being reported that confirms the importance of a nutritious diet in skin and hair health—information that may be different from what you have heard in the past. Your skin and hair require nourishment—the vitamins, minerals, lipids, and other nutrients that healthy foods provide. Most experts say that a healthy diet can improve the health of your skin and hair from the inside out, so think about that the next time you go grocery shopping or are planning a meal. An easy way to remember good nutritional choices is to strive for "colorful" meals. This means emphasizing eating fruits and vegetables and unprocessed foods to whatever degree is workable for you. If you are a parent, this has the added benefit of teaching your children about the importance of healthy eating.

And speaking of what you put in your body, don't forget to drink lots of water. One cause of dry, flaking skin is dehydration. If your body is not well hydrated, your skin and hair will show it. Skin needs moisture to be healthy, and so does the rest of your body. Drinking plenty of water will help. Consider adding more water to your daily routine and reducing your intake of soda and coffee.

Sleep Hygiene

Let's face it: Most of us don't get enough sleep. In this day and age it can take tremendous discipline to shut down the computer, put away your smart phone, and turn off the TV an hour or more before bedtime. But this could be an important step in your efforts to recover from your BFRB.

Late evenings are among the most vulnerable times for pulling and picking, especially when you are alone. What can you do instead? As bedtime approaches, consider engaging in a healthy grooming routine, dimming the lights, and doing light reading, gentle stretching, or crafts or artwork that keep your hands and mind engaged. Allowing your nervous system to settle down so you're better prepared for sleep will help you be better able to enjoy a pull-free or pick-free evening. If possible, try not to stay up when everyone else has gone to bed. If you think, *I'll just stay up for a few extra minutes*, recognize that this is likely to be a mistaken belief or a self-deception within the Cognitive domain. In your heart you know that once you start, it probably won't be just a few minutes! When you lose sleep to your BFRB, you may be losing two or three hours of sleep during which time your body could have been repairing itself and your mind could have been getting a well-earned rest. The term beauty sleep is not just a throwaway phrase!

Physical Exercise

You already know that physically activity is good for your general health, but it can also contribute to the success of your self-help program. When people exercise, the skin perspires, which invigorates and stimulates the skin and flushes out the pores. Use gentle exfoliation products while bathing or showering afterwards, followed by moisturizers that will hydrate and nourish your skin. As an additional benefit, clean, damp, and conditioned hair is not as attractive a target for many hair pullers.

SELF-REGULATION OF EMOTIONS AND INTERNAL FEELINGS

Good grooming habits are a great beginning, but as you have seen, there is more to explore on the path to wellness. At this point, let's look at the mind-body connection and how that relates to your ComB program.

As we have previously discussed, many of you may find that you are more vulnerable to picking or pulling when you are experiencing stressful emotions, such as frustration, anxiety, boredom, or anger. It is widely known that people who struggle with difficult emotional states can benefit from certain mind-body exercises. So it should be no surprise that these exercises may also improve your life in other ways.

There are many potentially helpful exercises available online, in books, and on DVDs or CDs that can help manage stress and other uncomfortable emotional states. What follows are short descriptions of a few of them. You can find more information in the "Resources and References" section at the end of this book. Most of the exercises below include a mindfulness component, involving states of nonjudgmental awareness. We have selected these approaches because they are relatively simple, take only brief amounts of time, and have been shown in good clinical research to provide emotional and behavioral advantages to their users. As you read about them, we would like you to consider trying at least one of them for ten or more minutes at a time (for most, working up to fifteen or twenty minutes is ideal), several times a week. Once they are part of your routine, we think you will enjoy them. Maybe even tell yourself that before you pick or pull, you will engage in one of the following activities first. This will buy you time, and might help break the BFRB cycle. In addition to contributing to your recovery, these simple exercises also have the potential to improve your general well-being.

Body Scan Exercise

Mindful awareness of the sensations your body is producing is a good way to increase awareness of your body and the impact that different mental and physical states have on you. This practice is easiest to do lying down with your eyes closed and is a good way to relax in the evening before going to bed. It can also be done when waking up, to help you clear your head before tackling the tasks of the day. As its name implies, it involves taking an inventory of your body's physical sensations (for example, tingling, itching, heaviness, pressure, and even urges to pick or pull) in a systematic way, without judging or trying to force them away. By doing so, you allow yourself to notice areas of discomfort, while also noticing the parts of your body that are not uncomfortable. In addition, you gain practice in experiencing sensations while trying to refrain from reacting to them emotionally, judging them, or acting on them. This can be especially important for your BFRB recovery program.

Note that you are not necessarily trying to decrease pain, discomfort, or muscle tension, although this often happens spontaneously. But some versions of the exercise include "breathing through" the body's areas of discomfort, which, in turn, can allow those areas to let go of unwanted sensations and to relax. This can be particularly helpful if it is employed when you are experiencing urges to pick or pull.

Mindful Awareness of the Breath, Emotions, and Thoughts

These exercises focus on increasing nonjudgmental awareness of the vast array of ever-changing physical, mental, and emotional states that come and go throughout each day. The first is mindful awareness of breathing. This exercise is a fundamental part of most mindfulness and meditation practices, but you can also use it as a "stand-alone" practice. In essence, the goal is to focus on your breath without trying to control or change it. As is the case with the body scan, you acknowledge the sensations that are associated with your breathing, breath by breath. It is expected that your mind will wander, and when it does so you can practice noticing this, and then return your attention to your breath as best you can, even if those distractions return or remain in the background. If you find it useful, you can count your breaths to help you keep your focus, but this is not necessary. In fact, it is the awareness that you have "drifted," and your ability to return to the breath without judging yourself, that are most important, even if this is possible only a small percentage of the time. You will get better at that with more practice.

Mindful awareness of the breath can be expanded to include other internal states as well. Whatever "bubbles up"—images, thoughts, emotions, or varieties of sensations—the idea is to notice them—recognize that they are present at that moment. Allow yourself to experience them without judging them, and notice how they change and eventually move on as others take their place as the objects of your attention. The gentle willingness to observe your internal experiences in an honest, nonjudgmental way, and trusting that they are only a small part of you, and not the most important part—this experience can provide a sense of peace, clarity, and self-compassion. This exercise can be an excellent tool for managing feelings of stress, upsetness, frustration, or anxiety; in other words, emotions associated with the Affective domain. Furthermore, even though these are not "problem-solving" exercises, many people report that solutions to problems spontaneously emerge during or following these practices.

Gentle Physical Exercise

Physical exercise has long been recognized as having the potential to help people, not only physically, but mentally as well. The good news is that these benefits are not only for those who live physically active lives, but they also apply to those whose lives involve more gentle exercises such as doing daily chores, walking, stretching, or practicing yoga.

There are many varieties of yoga, yet all of them emphasize the importance of mindful awareness of the body as you slowly stretch, bend, and hold certain physical positions in stillness as you go through a sequence of postures. Don't think of it as the latest fad—yoga has been around for thousands of years. Yoga exercises can be done in as little as ten minutes each day, although longer sessions are considered by some to be optimal. If you choose to try this option, try to build up to it over time. There are a number of books available, CDs to listen to, and videos to watch that will guide you through yoga practice. Actually attending a yoga class led by a knowledgeable instructor will ensure that your practice is appropriate to your age and physical condition—in addition to being more fun socially, as you join others in the same practice!

Other forms of low-impact physical exercise, such as walking, have been shown to produce a greater sense of well-being and lower levels of depression than sedentary activities, such as watching television or doing deskwork. In addition to ordinary walking, you might enjoy "mindful walking meditation," where you walk slowly, carefully, and with openness to all aspects of your experience. This kind of walking increases your awareness of sensations associated with movement, pressure, sounds, sights, and other elements in the environment as you focus on each moment and each step.

Clinical research has found that walking at a normal or brisk pace is also beneficial, especially when it is done in a natural setting. The popularity of public parks, beaches, mountain trails, and other environments that allow us to get close to nature's bounty is testament to the value of these environments: they provide many sensory, physical, psychological, and even spiritual benefits that we may not otherwise experience. As a bonus, being in fresh air is good for your skin!

We recognize that practicing these exercises will involve a certain amount of time and effort, but we believe that they can be valuable components of your recovery plan and your life. If the healthful exercises described here don't appeal to you, there are many others that you can find online, in books, and elsewhere. We are confident that if you keep looking you will find an approach—or combination of approaches—that is just right for you.

GET ACCURATE INFORMATION FROM HEALTH PROFESSIONALS

At some point during your self-help program you may want to discuss your hair or skin concerns, and their relationship to your general health, with health care professionals. In addition, much information and advice about health is available on the Internet, but be sure to go to reputable websites, such as Medline or the Mayo Clinic websites. We also encourage you to check out the TLC Foundation website for articles written by experts regarding hair and skin care, and products relevant to your recovery.

In some cases, professional interventions may be desirable or necessary. This is because professionals have access to more effective medications and utilize therapy techniques that are not available to the general public. In addition, they help limit further damage by knowing when additional measures are ill advised. Many dermatologists and other professionals now offer laser hair removal, electrolysis, microblading, dermabrasion, and other therapeutic techniques that can remove unwanted hair, fill in bare areas, and help restore skin health. Before committing to a course of treatment, we advise you to do your homework and get details about what is involved, the cost, and any potential side effects.

TRY IT!   Now that you have completed your initial *Action Plan*, take it out and have a look at what you have planned. Is there any room to include one or more of the recommendations in this chapter? If so, why not go ahead and write it in? Consider it to be a wellness component added to your recovery plan. After all, this is the first day of the rest of your life!

Conclusion

We hope that integrating the ComB model into a bigger wellness picture resonates with you. Your physical, mental, and emotional health are intertwined. In fact, it is possible that your picking or pulling has actually discouraged you from engaging in some of the activities recommended above because you don't feel that you have the time, energy, or confidence to follow through with them. We recommend that you not wait until you have made a full recovery to pursue those that might appeal to you. Instead, choose one or more of the recommendations and put them in your life now. This would be creating a positive chain of events to replace some unhelpful ones: you begin doing yoga or walking, which makes you feel energized and contributes to your feeling of well-being. Being physically active makes you a little more tired at night, so you go to bed earlier instead of staying up late and picking or pulling. When you get more sleep, you feel better and look better. This will remind you that you are worth taking good care of, and that can give you more confidence to take your ComB *Action Plan* to heart.

In parting, we encourage you to continue to use this book as a resource, coming back to it as often as you wish—when you need reminders, support, or ideas to get through tough or tempting times. It takes a diligent effort to prevail in the face of life's (and our own) imperfections. But as the billionaire and philanthropist Andrew Carnegie said, "Anything in life worth having is worth working for." We can think of no better use of time, energy, and effort than for you to create your own version of a healthy, happy life in the places where your BFRB once ruled.

So best wishes from us as you continue toward the recovery that you deserve and a life in which your suffering is minimal, and your joy is boundless!

Acknowledgements

This book could not have been written without the support of many individuals and organizations. We would like to take this opportunity to gratefully acknowledge them.

First, we want to thank our families for the tolerance and good humor they demonstrated during this long process. We are aware that our preoccupation with this project created hardships for them, and we appreciate their unflagging support.

We would also like to thank our friends and colleagues at the TLC Foundation for Body-Focused Repetitive Behaviors for their dedication to improving the lives of those who suffer from BFRBs, and for providing us with the joy and satisfaction of being part of this organization from its very beginning. Our involvement with TLC over the years has been—and remains—an invaluable experience for us.

Our heartfelt thanks are extended to Christina Pearson, Founding Director of the TLC Foundation and Visionary Director of the Heart and Soul Academy, for inspiring thousands of sufferers and their families for many years. She is a remarkable person who has affected our lives, both personally and professionally. She continues to enrich us with her wisdom, experience, and mere presence! For that we are most grateful.

We are indebted to our colleagues at the Behavior Therapy Center of Greater Washington, who, as providers of effective and compassionate care for those who suffer with BFRBs, exemplify the potential that we hope increasing numbers of therapists will provide.

We also thank the editors at New Harbinger Publishers, Ryan Buresh, Caleb Beckwith, and Ken Knabb, who skillfully shepherded us through the process of bringing our vision to fruition. We also extend our appreciation to New Harbinger's layout, technical, and design staff, whose attention to detail and to the visual elements of the layout and the cover have brought our book to life.

And we offer our special thanks to Jennifer Raikes, the Executive Director of the TLC Foundation, for writing the forward to our book. She has done so much to ensure that TLC remains a dynamic force in advancing the cause of BFRB sufferers everywhere. Jen has been an inspiration and joy for us to work with for many years.

Forms and Interventions

BLANK FORMS

(Note: Larger, more usable copies of these forms are available from the New Harbinger website: www.newharbinger.com/43645.)

Self-Monitoring Form

Where and What:

When:

	S C A M P
	S C A M P
	S C A M P
	S C A M P

What I did with the "product":

First aware of urge/behavior (0-4):	**Amount that I picked or pulled (0-4):**
0 = Entering situation, 4 = Mid to late in episode	0 = None, 4 = Extreme

Comments:

Action Plan							
Situation (Location/Activity):							
When Started:							
Interventions (Circle Relevant Domain Letters)	S	M	T	W	T	F	S
Problem: Intervention: S C A M P							
Problem: Intervention: S C A M P							
Problem: Intervention: S C A M P							
Problem: Intervention: S C A M P							
Awareness (0-4) 0 = Entering setting 4 = Mid to late in episode							
How much did I pick or pull? (0-4) 0 = None, 4 = Extreme							
Comments:							

SHORT LIST OF INTERVENTIONS

(Note: A much longer "Master List of Interventions" is available on the New Harbinger website: www.newharbinger.com/43645.)

The Sensory Domain

Fidget items

Scalp massager

Receive a massage

Brush hair

Use eye ointment on eyelashes

Manipulate silky fabric swatches

Floss teeth (oral stimulation)

Chew gum

Nibble on snack food

Knead silly putty, play dough, clay

Use skin care, hair care, or nail care products

Manipulate hand toys (Koosh ball, pipe cleaners, worry beads, stones, etc.)

Use Cortisone and other medicinal creams on site

Use soft brush or feather on face, lips, brows, etc.

The Cognitive Domain

Sample Healthy Thoughts to Challenge Cognitions That Maintain Your BFRB:

Who am I kidding? Besides, having imperfect skin/hair is better than the mess I am making of my own doing.

In my heart, I know I will only make things worse.

I have to accept that regrowth will probably be uneven or imperfect and may not look as good as I hope, especially in the beginning, but it will look and feel better over time. And even if the new growth is never perfect, I can live with it.

How often do I stop after a minute or after just one? Answer: Never!

Urges don't really last forever. When I get my plan into place I will see that urges come and go.

Picking or gouging will lead to more blood and scars and just make things worse.

No excuses! I have to find ways to become more aware so I can heal.

I should know by now that willpower alone is not going to solve my problem.

I need to be patient and stick with it. There are always new ideas for me to use. I'll try to learn from my setbacks and start fresh each day.

The Affective Domain

Deep breathing

Relaxation exercise

Scheduling pleasurable activities

Scheduling relaxation times

Meditation, yoga

Daily gratitude lists

Effective communication/Assertiveness

Positive visualization

Journal writing

Medications

Exercise, volunteer work

Acceptance, use of affirmations

Talking things over with friends or confidants

The Motor Domain

Play with "fiddle toys."

Cover fingertips with medical tape.

Wear finger bandages.

Wear glasses.

Wear a hat/bandana/headband.

Wear elbow brace.

Wear light cotton gloves.

Wear false eyelashes or makeup.

Tape/bandage on picking site.

Wear driving gloves.

Wear clothes that cover the picking.

Cut fingernails short.

Get short haircut.

Keep hands moist with lotion.

Groom nails.

Engage in knitting or other crafts.

Engage in physical exercise.

Wear a wig or hairpiece.

Keep hands away from BFRB site.

Clench your fists.

The Place Domain

Remove or cover mirrors.

Put "Caution" sign on bathroom door.

Eliminate tweezers.

Eliminate magnifying mirrors.

Dim lights while toileting.

Put a timer in the bathroom.

Put sticky note reminders on mirrors.

Stay out of certain rooms.

Keep "fiddle toys" in pulling location.

Ask for help.

Plan "busy work" for high-risk times.

Watch TV at low-risk times.

Avoid being alone in high-risk situations.

Plan "wind-down" before bedtime.

Resources and References

ORGANIZATIONS

TLC Foundation for Body-Focused Repetitive Behaviors
716 Soquel Avenue, Suite A, Santa Cruz, CA 95062
Phone: 831-457-1004
Fax: 831-427-5541
www.bfrb.org
info@bfrb.org

Heart and Soul Academy for BFRB Living Skills
Director: Christina Pearson
Phone: 970-697-9677
https://hasacademy.org
info@hasacademy.org
Video:www.youtube.com/watch?v=kUNB3Dp8YCQ&feature=
youtu.be

International OCD Foundation
P.O. Box 961029, Boston, MA 02196
Phone: 617-973-5801
Fax: 617-507-0495
https://iocdf.org/
info@iocdf.org

Anxiety and Depression Association of America (ADAA)
8701 Georgia Avenue, Suite 412, Silver Spring, MD 20910
Phone: 240-485-1001
Fax: 240-485-1035
https://adaa.org
information@adaa.org

PUBLICATIONS

Books

Golomb, R. G., and S. M. Vavrichek. 2000. *The Hair Pulling "Habit" and You: How to Solve the Trichotillomania Puzzle. Revised edition.* Silver Spring, MD: Writers' Cooperative of Greater Washington.

Kabat-Zinn, J. 2013. *Using the Wisdom of Your Body and Mind to Face Stress, Pain, and Illness. Revised edition.* New York: Bantam Books.

Mouton-Odum, S., and R. G. Golomb. 2013. *A Parent Guide to Hair Pulling Disorder: Effective Parenting Strategies for Children with Trichotillomania.* Silver Spring, MD: Goldum Publishing.

Articles

Flores, D. M. 2014. "SCAMP to skin picking recovery." *In Touch: A TLC Publication* 74: 1, 8–10.

Golomb, R. G., and C. S. Mansueto. 1994. "Trichotillomania in children." *In Touch: A TLC Publication* 2: 1, 7–8.

Oaklander, M. 2017. "Simple moves can lead to a less stressed-out you." *Time*, February 6: 56.

Panza, G. A., B. A. Taylor, P. D. Thompson, C. M. White, and L. S. Pescatello. 2017. "Physical activity intensity and subjective well-being in healthy adults." *Journal of Health Psychology.* DOI: 10.1177 /1359105317691589.

For Professionals

Azrin, N. H., and R. G. Nunn. 1973. "Habit reversal: A method of eliminating nervous habits and tics." *Behaviour Research and Therapy* 11: 619–628.

Falkenstein, M. J., S. Mouton-Odum, C. S. Mansueto, R. G. Golomb, and D. A. F. Haaga. 2016. "Comprehensive behavioral (ComB) treatment of trichotillomania: A treatment development study." *Behavior Modification* 40: 414–438.

Golomb, R., M. Franklin, J. E. Grant, N. J. Keuthen, C. S. Mansueto, S. Mouton-Odum, C. Novak, and D. Woods. 2011. *Expert Consensus Treatment Guidelines for Trichotillomania, Skin Picking and Other Body-Focused Repetitive Behaviors.* Santa Cruz, CA: Scientific Advisory Board of the Trichotillomania Learning Center.

Mansueto, C. S. In press. "Comprehensive behavioral (ComB) treatment for trichotillomania (hair pulling disorder) and excoriation (skin picking) disorder." In G. Todd and R. Branch, *Evidence-Based Treatment for Anxiety Disorders and Depression: A Cognitive Behavior Therapy Compendium*. New York: Oxford University Press.

Mansueto, C. S. 2013. "Trichotillomania (hair pulling disorder): Conceptualization and treatment." *Independent Practitioner* 4: 120–127.

Mansueto, C. S., R. G. Golomb, A. M. Thomas, and R. M. Stemberger. 1999. "A comprehensive model for the behavioral treatment of trichotillomania." *Cognitive and Behavioral Practice* 6: 23–43.

Mansueto, C. S., R. M. Stemberger, A. M. Thomas, and R. G. Golomb. 1997. "Trichotillomania: A comprehensive behavioral model." *Clinical Psychology Review* 17: 567–577.

Stein, D. J., D. W. Woods, and N. J. Keuthen (Eds.). 2012. *Trichotillomania, Skin Picking and Other Body-Focused Repetitive Behaviors*. Arlington, VA: American Psychiatric Publishing, Inc.

Charles S. Mansueto, PhD, is founder and director of the Behavior Therapy Center of Greater Washington, a leading center for the treatment of obsessive-compulsive and related disorders. He has over thirty-five years of experience providing cognitive behavior therapy (CBT) for a broad range of clinical problems. He has written extensively and presented nationally and internationally on obsessive-compulsive disorder (OCD) and related disorders. He is past president and currently serves as a member of the Scientific Advisory Board of The TLC Foundation for Body-Focused Repetitive Behaviors. He is also a member of the Scientific and Clinical Advisory Board of the International OCD Foundation (IOCDF); and of OCD Mid-Atlantic, an IOCDF affiliate. He retired as a tenured professor of psychology after thirty-six years in the University System of Maryland.

Sherrie Mansfield Vavrichek, LCSW-C, is a senior clinician at the Behavior Therapy Center of Greater Washington. She specializes in CBT for body-focused repetitive behavior (BFRB) and a wide range of clinical problems. She integrates mindfulness, meditation, and Buddhist philosophy in her CBT practice and in her life. She is author of *The Guide to Compassionate Assertiveness*, and coauthor of *The Hair Pulling "Habit" and You*. She has presented at national conferences on numerous mental health topics, including compassionate assertiveness.

Ruth Goldfinger Golomb, LCPC, is a senior clinician with the Behavior Therapy Center of Greater Washington. She has specialized in providing CBT for people with a wide range of clinical disorders since the mid-eighties. She is a member of The TLC Foundation for Body-Focused Repetitive Behaviors Scientific Advisory Board. She regularly presents at professional workshops, meetings, and conferences. She is coauthor of *The Hair Pulling "Habit" and You*, *Stay Out of My Hair*, and *Psychological Interventions for Children with Sensory Dysregulation*.

Foreword writer **Jennifer Raikes** is executive director of The TLC Foundation for Body-Focused Repetitive Behaviors. She grew up with trichotillomania (hair pulling disorder), and is an award-winning documentary filmmaker whose film, *Bad Hair Life*, aired on public television.

MORE BOOKS *from*
NEW HARBINGER PUBLICATIONS

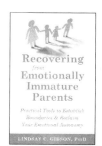

THE ANXIOUS THOUGHTS WORKBOOK

Skills to Overcome the Unwanted Intrusive Thoughts that Drive Anxiety, Obsessions & Depression

978-1626258426 / US $19.95

RECOVERING FROM EMOTIONALLY IMMATURE PARENTS

Practical Tools to Establish Boundaries & Reclaim Your Emotional Autonomy

978-1684032525 / US $16.95

THE MINDFULNESS WORKBOOK FOR OCD

A Guide to Overcoming Obsessions & Compulsions Using Mindfulness & Cognitive Behavioral Therapy

978-1608828784 / US $22.95

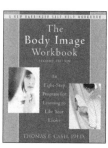

THE DIALECTICAL BEHAVIOR THERAPY SKILLS WORKBOOK, SECOND EDITION

Practical DBT Exercises for Learning Mindfulness, Interpersonal Effectiveness, Emotion Regulation & Distress Tolerance

978-1684034581 / US $24.95

THE BODY IMAGE WORKBOOK, SECOND EDITION

An Eight-Step Program for Learning to Like Your Looks

978-1572245464 / US $25.95

MINDFULNESS-BASED STRESS REDUCTION WORKBOOK, SECOND EDITION

978-1684033553 / US $25.95

Register your **new harbinger** titles for additional benefits!

When you register your **new harbinger** title—purchased in any format, from any source—you get access to benefits like the following:

- Downloadable accessories like printable worksheets and extra content
- Instructional videos and audio files
- Information about updates, corrections, and new editions

Not every title has accessories, but we're adding new material all the time.

Access free accessories in 3 easy steps:

1. Sign in at NewHarbinger.com (or **register** to create an account).

2. Click on **register a book**. Search for your title and click the **register** button when it appears.

3. Click on the **book cover or title** to go to its details page. Click on **accessories** to view and access files.

That's all there is to it!

If you need help, visit:

NewHarbinger.com/accessories

new harbinger
CELEBRATING
40 YEARS